JOURNAL FOR THE STUDY OF THE OLD TESTAMENT SUPPLEMENT SERIES

86

Editors
David J A Clines
Philip R Davies

JSOT Press
Sheffield

THE SYNTAX OF THE VERB IN CLASSICAL HEBREW PROSE

Alviero Niccacci

Translated by
W.G.E. Watson

Journal for the Study of the Old Testament
Supplement Series 86

Translated from the Italian
Sintassi del verbo ebraico nella prosa biblica classica
(Jerusalem: Franciscan Printing Press, 1986)
by arrangement with the publishers.

Published by JSOT Press
JSOT Press is an imprint of
Sheffield Academic Press Ltd
The University of Sheffield
343 Fulwood Road
Sheffield S10 3BP
England

Typeset by Sheffield Academic Press
and
Printed in Great Britain
by Billing & Sons Ltd
Worcester

British Library Cataloguing in Publication Data

Niccacci, Alviero
    The syntax of the verb in Classical Hebrew prose.
    —(JSOT supplement series, ISSN 0309-0787; 86)
    1. Hebrew language. Syntax
    I. Title II. Series   III. Sintassi del verbo ebraico nella prosa
    biblica classica. *English*
    492.4'5

    ISBN 1-85075-226-5

CONTENTS

FOREWORD

As I had to take over teaching Hebrew syntax for the degree course in the 'Studium Biblicum Franciscanum' from the late lamented Father Angelo Lancellotti who died prematurely on 19th March, 1984, I was faced with the unattractive prospect of having to present the subject in a way which even at the time of my own early studies at the end of the sixties I had considered to have little credibility. Since then I have become aware that the syntax of the verb is particularly fraught with problems. While it is true that Hebrew had only a limited number of verb forms at its disposal, it still seemed odd that, for example, WAYYIQTOL could be translated by virtually all the finite tenses of modern languages, as would appear from classical grammars. Nor is it easy to accept the view that QATAL, which was supposed to be the form for beginning narrative in Hebrew, could have been replaced so often in position by the WAYYIQTOL by customary misuse. It was obvious to me that the lengthy catalogues of special cases and exceptional uses listed in the grammars only show how difficult the problem is. In turn, translators select the equivalent tenses of modern languages somewhat at random, applying their own interpretation and sensitivity.

While looking for a solution which I could offer my students I came across two review articles by E. Talstra (Talstra I and II) and, in consequence, the work he reviewed. This was W. Schneider's grammar, an unpretentious class text book which has gone almost unnoticed by scholars. To give just one example, the broad spectrum of research on the Hebrew verbal system sketched by L. McFall (*The Enigma of the Hebrew Verbal System*, Sheffield, 1982) stops at 1954 (T. W. Thacker, *The Relationship of the Semitic and Egyptian Verbal Systems*, Oxford) in the conviction that nothing of significance appeared after that date.

The truth is that Schneider has opened the way for an approach to the problem which I believe to be correct. The solution he proposes is not synchronic but diachronic in character and instead of considering the origins of verbal forms in isolation it is concerned with their actual use and function in a text. Schneider has adopted the theoretical model of 'text linguistics' based on modern European languages developed by H. Weinrich and applied it to Hebrew. Now, text linguistics suggests an approach to the problem of the Hebrew verb which promises to be more effective than the traditional approach. Regardless of its origin in terms of diachronic level and comparative linguistics, a verb form needs to be studied in texts, not in isolation but in connection with all its associated linguistic markers. Which modern tense should be used to translate it can be determined only when its function in the text has been understood. Schneider's grammar, therefore, seems to me to be a first step in the right direction. His insistence on purely morphological and linguistic principles in determining the function of verb forms is surely welcome. Just as welcome, though, is Talstra's reminder not to forget the semantic principle which is subordinate to the other principles but still necessary.

I consider Schneider's application of the Weinrich model to be at an incomplete stage as yet. Accordingly, I have tried to go a little further, venturing into the area of 'tense shifts' in Hebrew in order to trace out a broader picture which is both structured and consistent. One more difference in approach between my researches and those of Schneider and Talstra needs to be emphasized. In order to arrive at fairly clear results I have considered it necessary to study prose separately from poetry. Poetry has its own rules concerning the use of tense and, unfortunately, they are still mysterious; they cannot be derived from prose and vice versa. My basis, therefore, is extensive reading of good narrative texts. In addition, comparison between parallel passages has often proved illuminating with regard to the various means of expression in Hebrew. In this connection I can say that A. Bendavid's *Parallels in the Bible* (Jerusalem, 1972) is a valuable 'handbook' for the study of Hebrew. The present 'Syntax of the verb', therefore, is the result of my reading up to now. Scrutiny of a wider selection of texts might contribute further refinements but I do not envisage major modifications.

In all likelihood the present contribution, like Schneider's, will incur scepticism from some scholars. The strongest criticism will probably concern the syntactic nature of QATAL. It will become clear, though, that contrary to common opinion it is not a narrative verb form except in a few cases which belong to the special construction I call the 'two-member syntactic construction'. In this respect the criterion of word-order in the clause is important as is, therefore, the syntactic value of 'first position in the sentence'.

In the first two chapters I summarize the basic principles of 'text linguistics' (Weinrich) with some reference to the application of these principles to Hebrew (Schneider). Chapters 3 and 4 provide an outline of the solution proposed. Should this book be used for teaching, the teacher must make sure that the students have mastered the material before proceeding further. To achieve this it would be helpful to combine theory with extensive and continuous readings of narrative in order to show how the principles described actually apply in contexts which are longer and less disjointed than those I have provided.

Chapters 5 and 6, then, examine in more detail the two fundamental linguistic categories of prose—narrative and speech—which correspond to what Weinrich calls 'linguistic attitude'. In Chapter 7 I provide a systematic classification of the forms and constructions in Hebrew which correspond to the other two aspects also formulated by Weinrich: 'linguistic perspective' and 'emphasis'. It will become evident that even though the two basic categories, narrative and speech or comment, are clearly defined by typical forms and verbal constructions as well as by characteristic linguistic markers, they do not behave as if they were two unconnected monolithic blocks. On the contrary, mixed categories do occur (identified chiefly with the help of morphological, syntactic and semantic criteria) which I term 'comment in the guise of narrative', 'narrative discourse' and 'narrative comment'.

Up to this point I have considered, for the most part, the individual sentence with all its linguistic components in order to explain how its individual forms and verbal constructions work. In Chapter 8 I switch my attention to inter-sentence relationships. For at least a partial study of this virtually unexplored topic (F.I. Andersen, *The Sentence in Biblical Hebrew*, The Hague, Paris & New York, 1974) which is admittedly difficult to study, I analyse the 'two-member syntactic construction' (protasis-apodosis). It will be seen that this pattern exhibits such a gamut of constructions, each the equivalent of the other, that it comprises a special observation-point. There is still a great deal yet to be explained, though, particularly concerning parataxis in both categories (narrative and speech). The difficulty lies in finding reliable criteria (from morphology, syntax and semantics) to determine when a form or verbal construction is simply continuative and when it is 'inverted' instead. The reader will find some comments on this topic in the discussion of the volitional forms weYIQTOL and weQATAL (Chapter 6).

Chapter 9 is a deeper examination of the criteria for textlinguistic analysis, and also summarises the results of our research. Only at this point, after analysing the various syntactic settings suggested by a reading of the texts, has it been possible to identify the forms and verbal constructions which can exist independently within the Hebrew verbal system (WAYYIQTOL, QATAL, YIQTOL, weQATAL, weYIQTOL, the simple noun clause, the complex noun clause) and to extend the list of tenses for each. These equivalents are not dependent on the tense used in modern translations but on the function which a particular form or construction has in the text. Once the function has been identified it is possible to determine the exact tense to be used in translation.

Chapter 10 has been added as a supplement because I had decided to deal with the use of tense in poetry completely separately from prose. Obviously, a course of syntax must provide students with an introduction to reading poetic texts. My account, though, does no more than list the basic facts for the problem of the verb in Hebrew poetry, based on a few studies I consider to be important. Unfortunately, the fact remains that in contrast with prose, poetry offers a very limited number of linguistic markers for identifying the function of individual forms and verbal constructions in a text. As a result, the problems a scholar has to face are more complex.

This research work was undertaken for the school and is intended chiefly for the school. I decided to publish it because so few studies of Hebrew syntax are available, especially in Italian.

Jerusalem, 14th March 1986

Note to the English Edition

The text presented here in English translation is an extensive revision of the Italian original (published by the Franciscan Printing Press in 1986, 127 pages). The basic structure remains unchanged. Quite a number of changes to the text and to the footnotes have been included and examples have been added or replaced and various tables or figures inserted. The greatest changes are due to the need for specifying in more detail the three levels of text linguistics (linguistic attitude, prominence, linguistic perspective) in relation to Hebrew (Chapter 7, Tense Shift). I have also attempted to combine text linguistic analysis which functions at the level of the paragraph or longer units with grammatical analysis, which functions at the level of the individual sentence. As a result it has been possible to specify the functions of the compound nominal clause in relation to the verb clause (§§ 6.167) and to specify the syntactic significance of 'first position in the sentence' whether in the individual clause, the paragraph or the longer unit of text (§§ 126-127). Using these criteria it has been possible to classify all the verb forms and grammatical constructions in Hebrew and to identify each of their functions (§135). Furthermore, using textlinguistics, it has been possible to establish criteria for determining parataxis and hypotaxis in the relationships among the different types of clause (§ 95). Some improvement has also been made in the area of discourse analysis, which before was vastly inferior to the analysis of narrative. See especially § 55 for the x-indicative YIQTOL construction and § 135, No. 8 for weQATAL. The forms of discourse still require study, though, in particular the indirect volitional forms. Another important task is the analysis of adverbs and particles as macrosyntactic markers. Some discussion of this topic is to be found in the recent study B. Züber, *Das Tempussystem des biblischen Hebräisch*, Berlin & New York, 1986, pp. 156-84, even if his basic approach seems to be open to discussion.

On this aspect see my review in *LA* 36 (1986), pp. 397-405. In addition, once the difficulties posed by the single sentence and the paragraph have been resolved further research on longer units of narrative and discourse will be required. I have been able to achieve only very little in this area by examining Exodus 1-14 in terms of the text function of antecedent constructions and of *wayehi* (§ 36). In my opinion this analytical approach should be applied systematically to a wider range of texts.

As in the Italian edition I have accepted the biblical texts as they are without resorting to literary criticism or taking much notice of scholars who use this method. It is, in any case, a duty to presume that even the various kinds of 'glosses' or inserts also follow the rules of grammar and syntax. I think it injudicious to adopt the principle which unfortunately so many scholars follow that so-called 'difficulties' or 'mistakes' of grammar and syntax are indications of later reworking. In effect this would mean that the writers of such glosses either did not know the language or at the least were inept. I wish to reiterate here a caution against the danger of making syntax as arbitrary as literary criticism. On this topic see the book by Züber (pp. 19ff.) and my review (reference given above). I prefer to follow this method closely rather than 'correct' the texts using 'rules' even if difficult cases remain which require further study (see, for example, § 158-ii).

It is a pleasure to thank Dr W.G.E. Watson who suggested translating this booklet into English and after completing his first translation then took on the task of incorporating the not inconsiderable changes from the revised edition. I also thank him for the improvements in lay-out he suggested and for additional bibliographical references.

Jerusalem, 30th November 1987

Translator's note

Apart from the permanent problem of converting fluent Italian into readable English without too much distortion my chief difficulty has been to try and find acceptable equivalents for some recurrent technical terms. Many derive from Weinrich and are ultimately German; others have been coined by the author. They are as follows:

comment in the guise of narrative: *narrazione commentativa*
degree zero: *grado zero (Nullstufe)*
narrative comment/discourse: *commento/discorso narrativo*
past perfect: *trapassato*
present perfect: *passato prossimo*
prominence: *messa in rilievo (Reliefgebung)*; another possible equivalent is 'salience'
simple past: *passato prossimo*
tense shift: *transizione temporale (Tempus-Übergang)*
two-member syntactic construction: *schema sintattico a due membri*
volitive: *volitivo*; also possible would be 'volitional'

Morpeth, 28th September 1988

ABBREVIATIONS

a. *List of publications cited by abbreviation*

Bartelmus	R. Bartelmus, *HYH. Bedeutung und Funktion eines 'Allerweltswortes'*, St. Ottilien, 1982
Bendavid, II	A. Bendavid, *Biblical and Mishnaic Hebrew, Volume II: Grammar & Style*, Tel-Aviv, 1971 (in Hebrew)
Beyer	K. Beyer, *Semitische Syntax im Neuen Testament*, 2nd edn, Göttingen, 1968
Dahood, *Psalms*	M. Dahood, *Psalms, I-III*, Garden City, New York, 1965-1970
Gesenius–Kautzsch	*Gesenius' Hebrew Grammar*, as edited and enlarged by the late E. Kautzsch, 2nd English edition, revised... by E. Cowley, Oxford, 1960
Gross, *VTS* 32	W. Gross, 'Syntaktische Erscheinungen am Anfang althebräischer Erzählungen: Hintergrund und Vordergrund', *VTS* 32 (1981), pp. 131-45
Joüon	P. Joüon, *Grammaire de l'hébreu biblique*, Rome, 1923
Meyer, III	R. Meyer, *Hebräische Grammatik, III. Satzlehre* Berlin/New York 1972
Muraoka	T. Muraoka, *Emphatic Words and Structures in Biblical Hebrew*, Jerusalem & Leiden 1985
Richter, *Grundlagen*	W. Richter, *Grundlagen einer althebräischen Grammatik, I-III*, St. Ottilien, 1978-1980
Schneider	W. Schneider, *Grammatik des biblischen Hebräisch*, 5th edn, München, 1982
Talstra I	E. Talstra, 'Text Grammar and Hebrew Bible. I: Elements of a Theory', *BiOr* 35 (1978), pp. 169-74
Talstra II	E. Talstra, 'Text Grammar and Hebrew Bible. II: Syntax and Semantics', *BiOr* 39 (1982), pp. 26-38
Watson, *Classical Hebrew Poetry*	W.G.E. Watson, *Classical Hebrew Poetry. A Guide to its Techniques*, Sheffield, 1984
Weinrich	H. Weinrich, *Tempus. Le funzioni dei tempi nel testo*, Bologna, 1978

b. *In addition to the abbreviations used in Liber Annuus (LA) from 1980 on, note the following*

BHK	Biblia Hebraica, ed. R. Kittel
BHS	Biblia Hebraica Stuttgartensia, ed. K. Elliger and W. Rudolph
OTS	*Oudtestamentische Studiën*
MT	Masoretic Text

Chapter 1

THE PROBLEM OF TENSE IN HEBREW

§1. This is the main problem of Hebrew syntax. The five verb forms QATAL, weQATAL, YIQTOL, weYIQTOL and WAYYIQTOL, have been translated by nearly all the tenses of modern languages, by every mood (except by the imperative for WAYYIQTOL) and by both aspects or 'modes of action' (complete and incomplete).

McFall[1] has made a survey of the opinions put forward between 1827 (Ewald) and 1954 (Thacker). He examined ten different theories in all, which he grouped under six basic headings. Of these can be mentioned the earliest solution, proposed since the tenth century by Jews of mediaeval times and by classical grammarians such as Gesenius, Joüon, etc., which is that the verbal system is based on tense. Without WAW, QATAL usually denotes the past and YIQTOL usually denotes the future; preceded by WAW, their tenses are reversed ('conversive/inversive WAW').

Others still hold to the comparative-historical solution, already supported by Knudtzon, Bauer, Driver and Thacker—in different forms—chiefly on the basis of Akkadian. The twofold function of QATAL (with/without WAW) and of YIQTOL (with/without WAW) is explained by positing two originally different forms in Semitic: a stative QATAL denoting the present, an active QATAL denoting the past; a longer form of YIQTOL denoting the present/future and a shorter form of YIQTOL denoting the past. Alternatively the QATAL was supposed to have several functions while the YIQTOL was universal.

The discussion has even been extended to include the verbal systems of Ugaritic (§172) and, in the last few years, of Eblaite[2] but an acceptable solution is still far off.

Clearly this type of research must be diachronic. It is an attempt at explaining the Hebrew verbal system by tracing the origin of the different forms either in Proto-semitic or in the most ancient Semitic languages known. Any such solution, even if one acceptable to everyone is found, cannot replace a synchronic analysis intended to check the appropriate functions of the verb forms in the text (§130).

Chapter 2

A NEW APPROACH: TEXT LINGUISTICS

§2. According to H. Weinrich,[3] 'The formula "text linguistics" denotes a method used in linguistics to describe all the elements of a language including the function these have in oral and written texts. . . A grammar which does not accept units beyond the sentence can never even notice let alone resolve the most interesting problems of linguistics'.[4]

§3. From a detailed study of modern literary texts Weinrich was able to differentiate two sets of tenses with separate functions. Group I 'discourse' or 'comment'; Group II functioning as 'narrative'. The first or second persons are used chiefly in Group I, the third person in Group II.

Here is a list of the English verbal forms of the two groups, arranged according to the three basic axes of time.

axis	Discourse (Group I)	Narrative (Group II)
'present'	present	imperfect
'past'	present perfect	{ simple past { past perfect
'future'	future	conditional

Very perceptively, Weinrich considers these narrative texts from three aspects: linguistic attitude, foregrounding and linguistic perspective. Each of these leads to the discovery of different dimensions in such texts. For each of these dimensions I will indicate in the following tables the verb forms in English, following Weinrich's analysis and I will also add the corresponding Hebrew constructions (not dealt with by Weinrich), partly following Schneider (p. 5).

(1) Linguistic attitude: narrative, commentary

English	Narrative Group II	Discourse Group I
Hebrew	WAYYIQTOL WAW-x-QATAL	volitive forms simple nominal clause indicative x-YIQTOL weQATAL (x-)QATAL

(2) Emphasis (or highlighting): foreground, background

English⟍ Hebrew⟍	foreground	background
Narrative —	WAYYIQTOL	{imperfect {past perfect ——— {simple noun clause {complex noun clause {weQATAL
Discourse —	present volitive mood ——— volitive forms (x-)QATAL x-indicative YIQTOL simple noun clause	{circumstantial clauses {gerund, past participle ——— {WAX-simple noun clause {WAW-complex noun clause

(3) Linguistic perspective: retrieved information (flashback, 'antecedent' to the ensuing account), degree zero (the level of the story itself), anticipated information ('disclosure', reveals the end of the story).

Eng⟍ Heb⟍	Recovered information (↑)	degree zero (O)	anticipated information (↓)
Narr. —	past perfect ——— WAW-x-QATAL	{simple past {imperfect ——— WAYYIQTOL	conditional ——— YIQTOL

	present perfect	present volitive moods	future
Disc. --	x-QATAL	volitive forms (x-)QATAL x-indicative YIQTOL simple noun clause	YIQTOL[6] final clauses etc.

By arranging his material on different linguistic levels the writer shows his freedom and also his control over the events narrated.

§4. Another important element in Weinrich's analysis comprises 'tense shifts' (Chapter 7) which can be either homogeneous or heterogeneous. These shifts are based on the two groups already identified (I with the function of commentary, II with the function of narrative). A shift is homogeneous when one verb form changes to another at the same time linguistic level (indicated by the symbol ←→); it is heterogeneous when occurring between verb forms belonging to different linguistic levels (indicated by the symbol →) 'Homogeneous shifts guarantee the uniformity of a text, its textuality... Heterogeneous shifts contribute little or nothing to textuality. Even so they are required in order to modify the amount of information available to the listener.[7] A clear example of a heterogeneous shift is the change from narrative to dialogue (where the speakers mostly use the tenses proper to commentary).

Further on (§§79ff.) we shall return to the subject of tense shifting.

§5. Schneider's grammar[8] is new inasmuch as it applies Weinrich's linguistic theory to Hebrew and so stresses the importance of text. In fact, grammatical description should be based on units of text longer than single sentences. A description of syntax should take into account the various linguistic forms which accompany the process of information. A description of syntax (i.e. the function of the form of the text) should take precedence over semantic description (the meaning of the actual form). E. Talstra wrote a long review of Schneider's grammar[9] in which he fully accepted the author's basic approach, at the same time trying to place more value on semantics (and therefore on traditional grammars) without denying its subordinate role with respect to syntax. On this problem see §§132-133.

The notes which follow are based on a position similar to that of Schneider and Talstra. Chapters 3 and 4 (§§6-25) set out the basic criteria required for a correct approach to the problem of the use of verbal forms in classical Hebrew prose. The account will be based on the analysis of texts; theoretical evaluation will be reduced to a minimum. The other criteria used in the solution proposed here will be pointed out later (§§128-138) to avoid overloading the introductory section. I hope that by then the reader will be in a position to understand them better. From Chapter 5 on a detailed explanation of the use of verbal forms in biblical prose will be provided. Poetry will be discussed briefly at the end (Chapter 10).

Chapter 3

NARRATIVE AND COMMENT

a. *The noun clause and the verbal clause*[10]

§6. Before we can begin to analyse text (narrative and comment) the different types of individual clause have to be determined. The following definition, which follows the model of Arabic grammarians, is better suited to Hebrew syntax than the generally accepted definition: a verbal clause begins with a verb, a noun clause begins with a noun. A verbal clause tells us *what the subject does*, in other words, what the action is; a noun clause tells us *who the subject is*. If a noun is followed by a verb the noun clause is complex.[11] Gen. 3.13 is quoted in various grammars as an example of a complex nominal clause with the function of specifying the subject and not of providing information on the action as such.

Gen. 3.13b

הנחש השיאני

It is the serpent who tricked me

On the analogy of the x-QATAL construction of 'report' (§§22-23) we cannot, of course, rule out the interpretation of הנחש השיאני as a verbal clause: '(You should know that; or The truth is that) the serpent tricked me'. Even so, I maintain that analysis as a complex nominal clause is to be preferred on the basis of the question-and-answer pattern present in 3.11-13. Indeed, God asks for more information concerning Adam's deed:

Gen. 3.11b

המן־אעץ אשר צויתיך לבלתי אכל־ממנו אכלת

Did you perhaps eat from the tree from which I commanded you not to eat?

Instead, Adam replies by indicating another person as responsible, using a phrase which is clearly a CNC:

Gen. 3.12b

('casus pendens', §123) האשה אשר נתתה עמדי

היא נתנה־לי מן־העץ ואכל

The woman whom you placed beside me,
she it was who gave (fruit) from the tree and I ate.

Similarly, in the exchange with Eve, God's question concerning the deed she had done:

Gen. 3.13a

מה־זאת עשית

What have you done?

This is probably why Eve, too, tries to offload her own responsibility onto someone else and that is why the expression quoted above (Gen. 3.13b) is, in fact, a CNC.

The grammar by Gesenius–Kautzsch rejects this analysis[12] but concedes that 'verbal-clauses of this kind approximate closely in character to noun-clauses'.[13] Meyer agrees[14] even though he continues to call this kind of clause 'verbal'. The definition of the complex noun clause given above has also been criticised recently by various scholars.[15] However, it has in fact been confirmed by analysis of texts both in (1) discourse and in (2) narrative.

(1) The non-verbal character of a clause beginning with a noun is evident from a comparison of two similar sentences:

Josh. 24.17

('casus pendens') כי יהוה אלהינו

הוא המעלה אתנו ואת־אבותינו מארץ מצרים מבית עבדים

ואשר עשה לעינינו את־האתות הגדלות האלה

For Yahweh, our God,
he it is who caused us and our fathers to come up
from the land of Egypt and from the house of slaves
and who worked those great signs in front of our eyes.

and Judg. 6.8b

כה־אמר יהוה אלהי ישראל

אנכי העליתי אתכם ממצרים

So says Yahweh the God of Israel:
—It is I who made you come up from Egypt—

The equivalence of the two basic constructions seems clear to me from these two examples;

(1) הוא—המעלה
(2) (הוא)—אשר עשה
(3) אנכי—העלתי

In both examples the clause begins with an independent personal pronoun with emphatic function. After the pronoun, in Josh. 24.17 the participle, preceded by the definite article is followed by אשר QATAL; in Judg. 6.8b it is followed by simple QATAL. This means that the simple QATAL fills the slot equivalent to the article + participle or אשר QATAL. All three clauses, therefore, are noun clauses with the function of specifying the subject of the action. Another characteristic they have in common is the position of the independent personal pronoun at the head of the clause. If 'x' is used to mark this first element we can display the three constructions as follows:

(1) x—participle with article
(2) x—אשר + QATAL
(3) x—QATAL

Other examples of construction (1) are:

Deut. 3.22b

כי יהוה אלהיכם ('casus pendens')
הוא הנלחם לכם
For Yahweh is your God,
he it is who will fight for you;

or, with the personal pronoun replaced by a noun:

Deut. 3.21b

עיניך הראאת. . .
It is your eyes that have seen. . .

Deut. 11

2   לא את־בניכם . . .
(long detailed description up to v. 6)
7   כי עיניכם הראת
2 . . . not your children. . .
7 but yours were the eyes that saw (Yahweh's great deeds)

The equivalence of constructions (2) and (3) is confirmed by a comparison of 1 Chron. 21.17 with its parallel 2 Sam. 24.17:

1 Chron. 21.17

... וַאֲנִי־הוּא אֲשֶׁר־חָטָאתִי

It is I who have sinned. . . (i.e., not the people)

2 Sam. 24.17

הִנֵּה אָנֹכִי <u>חָטָאתִי</u>

אָנֹכִי <u>הֶעֱוֵיתִי</u>

It is I who have sinned,
it is I who have acted wickedly.

In addition it should be noted that a construction of type (3) occurs with YIQTOL instead of QATAL:

Gen. 24.7

יְהוָה אֱלֹהֵי הַשָּׁמַיִם ... ('casus pendens')

הוּא <u>יִשְׁלַח</u>

Yahweh, God of the heavens. . .
it is he who will send (his angel). . .

In the parallel passage, when Abram's servant relates the same thing to Laban, the independent personal pronoun is missing but the meaning of the clause remains unchanged:

Gen. 24.40

יְהוָה אֲשֶׁר־הִתְהַלַּכְתִּי לְפָנָיו יִשְׁלַח ...

It is Y, in whose presence I have walked, who will
send (his angel).

Deut. 3.28

הוּא יַעֲבֹר ...

וְהוּא יַנְחִיל ...

(Joshua) he it is who shall cross (in front of the people)
and it is he who shall cause (them) to inherit (the land).

In all the foregoing examples it is evident from the context that the predicate of the sentence is the personal pronoun or the noun in the head position, not the verb.

Much the same is true of the interrogative sentence. There, too, the emphasis falls on the person ('subject', but actually the predicate) and not on the verb (action). The person is represented in the question by the pronoun מִי, 'who?' and is then specified by name in the answer. Both the pronoun and the noun are placed first in the sentence which can, therefore, be represented by the formula x-

YIQTOL or x-QATAL as the case may be. Note, too, that in the answer the verb can be omitted, confirmation that it is not the predicate of the sentence.

Judg. 1

1	‎... מי יעלה־לנו
2	‎יהודה יעלה

1 Who will go up for us. . .?
2 It is Judah who shall go up.

Judg. 20.18

‎... מי יעלה־לנו
‎יהודה

Judg. 6.29

‎... מי עשה הדבר הזה
‎גדעון בן־יואש עשה הדבר הזה

Who has done this thing?
It is Gideon, son of Joash, who has done this thing.

Judg. 15.6

‎... מי עשה זאת
‎שמשון

Who did this?
Samson. . .

(2) All the examples we have looked at so far belong in the category of discourse. Further research will show whether the situation in narrative is similar. The corresponding constructions in narrative, where the emphasis is placed on the 'x' element (nominal or adverbial) which precedes the finite verb are (WAW-)x-QATAL (§48) and WAW-x-YIQTOL (§46). Once again these constructions cannot be described as verbal: they are nominal. CNC's therefore, since they do not denote the action itself but the subject or the object (when 'x' is not a proper name) or else the manner (when 'x' is an adverb) of the action proper.

If we now combine the discourse constructions (listed above) with those proper to narrative four basic types emerge:

| (1) x- article + participle ⎫ | SNC |
| (2) x- ‎אשר + QATAL ⎭ | |

| (3) x- QATAL ⎫ | CNC |
| (4) x- YIQTOL ⎭ | |

In these the element 'x' can be a noun (independent personal pronoun or noun) or an adverb (or the equivalent of an adverb = preposition + noun/suffix pronoun). Constructions (1) and (2) feature two nominalizations of the verb (participle and relative clause),[16] while (3) and (4) comprise two simple verb forms. The first two constructions comprise the simple nominal clause (noun + noun) where the first member ('x') is the predicate; the second two comprise the complex nominal clause (noun + finite verb) in which the first member ('x') is likewise the predicate.

It can accordingly be stated that the typical feature of the CNC is to have the finite verb in second position within the clause. Its function is to emphasize the element 'x' which precedes the finite verb (subject, object or circumstance of the act). Since it is in first position the 'x' element becomes the predicate of the clause. This is how the CNC can be clearly distinguished from a verbal clause, where the finite verb is in first position and so comprises the predicate. As will be seen later, cases where the CNC loses its primary emphatic function within the single clause (§126, 3-6) can be accounted for by reason of the acquisition of a new and superior function within a wider unit than the single clause. This new function is the marking of syntactic hypotaxis (cf. §95, types 2-3). In addition it should be noted that the construction with 'casus pendens' is to be carefully differentiated from the CNC even though at times they both appear to be identical (cf. §§124-125 for criteria for this differentiation). In my opinion the complexity of this syntactic situation is the reason why in most modern grammars the traditional definitions of verbal and nominal clauses continue to be maintained.

The conclusion to be drawn is that the definition given at the beginning is not only valid, it is the only definition which can explain the syntactic state of a clause with a finite verb in second position. At this point we can state our opinion concerning the traditional definition which runs as follows: a clause is verbal when the predicate is a finite verb and nominal when the predicate is a noun. For this definition to be valid it should also be specified that in Hebrew a finite verbal form is a predicate when it comes first in the clause. When, instead, it is preceded by an element of any kind (other than WAW) the verbal form is not the predicate and therefore the clause is nominal (CNC). For the syntactic significance of 'first position in the clause', which is fundamental throughout the present study, see §135.

(3) The foregoing analysis forces us to revise the current notions of 'subject' and 'predicate' in Hebrew. By definition, the 'subject' is the topic spoken about (usually a person or animate being) and the 'predicate' is what is said about the subject. Modern linguists term these two components of the clause 'topic' and 'comment' or 'reference' and 'predication' or 'theme' and 'rheme'.[17] Now the subject is a noun or noun equivalent ('noun-phrase') while the predicate is a verb ('verb-phrase'). According to modern linguists the 'noun-phrase' has first position in the sentence. It should be noted, however, that this statement does not suit Hebrew, for two reasons. First, in Hebrew the first position in the sentence is filled by the predicate, not by the subject. Second when a Hebrew sentence begins with a noun or an adverb the predicate is not identical with the verb but in actual fact with that noun or adverb. Accordingly, what is normally the 'subject' becomes the 'predicate' and vice versa.

This transformation is not exclusive to Hebrew as it occurs in other languages, ancient and modern. It is effected by nominalisation of the verbal form.[18] To this type belong the first two constructions in Hebrew, listed above:

(1) noun—article + participle
(2) noun—אשר + QATAL

Typically, in Hebrew there is a way to effect the change from 'subject' to 'predicate' without nominalisation of the verb. Instead, the noun is simply placed at the head of the sentence. To this type belong the other two constructions discussed above:

(3) noun—QATAL
(4) noun—YIQTOL

b. *Narrative and discourse*

§7. Narrative concerns persons or events which are not present or current in the relationship involving writer-reader and so the third person is used. In discourse, on the other hand, the speaker addresses the listener directly (dialogue, sermon, prayer).

In Hebrew, the verb-form used in narrative is WAYYIQTOL while YIQTOL is the dominant form in discourse. Accordingly, WAYYIQTOL and YIQTOL (not YIQTOL and QATAL as traditional grammars assume) are the basic forms of the verb used in Hebrew prose. This is because they have become identified with the opposition narrative sphere (WAYYIQTOL)—commentary or 'discourse' (YIQTOL). It follows that the value of these and associated verb forms (in terms of the two categories indicated) has to be deduced from examining texts as concrete linguistic entities, with due allowance for other associated indicators of syntax.

Traditional grammars, instead, ignore the linguistic context and list the tense equivalents for the different verbal forms (YIQTOL, QATAL, their inverted forms, coordinated forms etc.) in terms of translation into modern languages. We will come back to this problem later (§§129ff.).

§8. Typically, 'narrative' uses a WAYYIQTOL in first position (verb clause: §6). 'Discourse', on the other hand, exhibits more variety. Volitive forms can be used as well as x-indicative YIQTOL, the simple noun clause and QATAL (§3, 1).

QATAL can occur in both narrative and discourse, but in different ways. The QATAL: which has first position in the sentence is distinct from a second position QATAL. The first kind occurs in discourse (§§22-23) but never in narrative (§15). Instead, the other type is found in both narrative and discourse. Simply because it has second position in the sentence it does not denote degree zero of information but the motive or preceding circumstance (more clearly so when preceded by כי. אשר, etc.). As such, QATAL can be labelled, in Weinrich's terminology, a 'retrospective' verb form (§3, 3).

§9. Narrative develops by means of a chain of WAYYIQTOLs. When this chain is interrupted (that is, when a verb form is used which is not a WAYYIQTOL) it shows that the writer wishes to change the level of information from narrating events to his commentary on those same events (cf. also §§39ff.). For example, let us inspect Gen. 7.17-20:

vv. 17-18:	narrative, series of WAYYIQTOLs. Having provided the last item of information—'The waters...' (v. 18)—the author interrupts the series of WAYYIQTOLs and uses two complex noun clauses to comment on that item of information:
v. 19	והמים גברו מאד מאד
	Now the waters increased very considerably over the land and covered all the highest mountains there are under the heavens.

v. 20   חמש עשרה אמה מלמעלה גברו המים

For fifteen cubits above (the mountains) did the
waters grow and cover the mountains.

In two complex noun clauses, vv. 19-20, the author comments on the
rise of the waters (narrated with the use of WAYYIQTOL in v. 18,
wayyigberu) stressing the extent of the marvel: the water was deep
enough not only to cover the highest mountains but to bury them
under fifteen cubits! Note the absolute contrast in verb forms of the
same root:

Narrative	Comment
v. 18 ויגברו	
	v. 19 והמים גברו
	15 אמה . . . גברו המים v. 20
WAYYIQTOL	(WAW-)x-QATAL
= verb clause	= complex noun clause
= foreground	= background

Another good example is Gen. 4.2-5a:

2	(narrative: series of WAYYIQTOLs)
3	ויבא קין מפרי האדמה
4	והבל הביא גם־הוא מבכרות צאנו ומחלבהן
	וישע יהוה אל־הבל ואל־מנחתו
5	ואל־קין ואל־מנחתו לא שעה

Here, too, the author interrupts the WAYYIQTOL-chain twice in
order to emphasize the difference between Cain and Abel in respect
of both their sacrifice (vv. 3-4a) and God's reaction to it (vv. 4b-5).
The structure of this passage is evident from the following diagram
(note that → denotes a heterogeneous tense shift, §4):

ויבא קין	→	והבל הביא
וישע . . . אל־הבל	→	ואל־קין . . . לא שעה
WAYYIQTOL	→	WAW-x-QATAL
foreground	→	background)

If the author had continued the series of WAYYIQTOLs, the two
characters would have been introduced next to each other, like links
in the same chain. Instead, he wanted to emphasize the contrast
between them (also emphasized in the chiastic sequence of proper
names: Cain-Abel-Abel-Cain), which comprises the motive for the
event about to be narrated (fratricide).

The same contrast (and chiastic sequence of proper names) occurs in the next example (a 'brief independent narrative', §27 embedded within an antecedent, §36):

Exod. 1

5	ויהי כל־נפש ...	→		ויוסף היה...
6	וימת יוסף ...	→	7	ובני ישראל פרו ...
5 All the people were. . .				Joseph, instead, was. . .
6 Then Joseph died. . .				7 Instead the Israelites multiplied. . .

On this topic see also §42.

§10. On the basis of the preceding two samples we can already establish an important contrast between the verb forms: WAYYIQTOL is used to narrate an event, WAW-x-QATAL to comment on the event itself. In the two examples cited we have noted the transition from one form to the other (WAYYIQTOL → (WAW)-x-QATAL). This transition is typical of narrative (cf. §86).

§11. In discourse, instead the transition from weQATAL WAW-x-YIQTOL occurs, as in the following example:

Gen. 12.12

כי־יראו אתך המצרים
ואמרו אשתו זאת
<u>והרגו אתי</u>
<u>ואתך יחיו</u>

When they see you the Egyptians will say: 'She is his wife'.
Me they'll kill but you they'll allow to live.

The transition weQATAL → WAW-x-YIQTOL is typical of discourse but it also occurs in narrative when it approximates discourse ('comment' on an event narrated previously, cf. §46). This transition, typical of discourse, corresponds to the transition WAYYIQTOL → WAW-x-QATAL typical of narrative (§9, cf. §58); both are used to express contrast between two characters or events. The examples already given can be cited again:

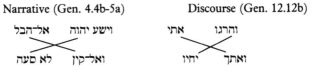

Narrative (Gen. 4.4b-5a)	Discourse (Gen. 12.12b)

WAYYIQTOL	= verb clause	weQATAL	= verb clause
	= foreground		= foreground
↓		↓	
WAW-x-QATAL	= comp. noun cl.	WAW-x-YIQTOL	= comp. noun cl.
	= background		= background

In each case the difference in the forms of the verb is combined with chiastic patterning (verb–object/object–verb) which emphasizes the contrast between the characters.

§12. Besides these typical verb forms, in narrative and discourse there are certain textual pointers, called 'macro-syntactic signs'. These are elements which mark the relationships among segments of the text. The main indicator of narrative is *wayehi* (§§28f.); *wehinneh* chiefly marks discourse but also functions in narrative, while *we'atta* is exclusive to discourse (§§67ff.). Mention should also be made here of *wehaya*, an important macrosyntactic marker in discourse which also occurs in the comment-sections of narrative. It will not be discussed directly here, but see §156.

The relationships among clauses in a text are indicated not only by such markers but also in several other ways, such as the use of pronouns (personal and demonstrative pronouns, etc.), particles and various conjunctions (§6).

§13. We can now specify the terminology adopted in the rest of these notes. The term 'narrative' presents no problems: it denotes a detached ('historical') account of events, as stated above (§7). The term 'discourse', however, needs some clarification. 'Discourse' also includes the 'comment' sometimes found within a narrative, when the writer holds up the story in order to relate his reflection on the events narrated or to define them in some way (cf. the examples given above: Gen. 7.17-20 and 4.2-4, §9). I will, however, use the term 'discourse', when the text addresses the listener directly, i.e. in discourse proper, dialogue, prayer, etc.; for all other cases I will use the term 'comment'.

It is appropriate to preserve this distinction in terminology because it goes hand in hand with a distinction in syntax. The very same verb forms correspond to different tenses in real 'discourse' and in 'comment' (narrative). For example, YIQTOL denotes the future in discourse (§52) but repeated action in comment (§34); the same applies to weQATAL (cf. §§55 and 46 respectively). In the same way the simple noun clause denotes the present in discourse (§53) but a contemporaneous action in comment (§?43). For a full discussion see §135.

Chapter 4

WAYYIQTOL AND QATAL

§14. In broad terms QATAL can be described as a verb form functioning retrospectively, used in narrative and in discourse, but in different ways. Generally, it is not a narrative form, in spite of what most grammars say (but cf. §148), unlike WAYYIQTOL, precisely because instead of being used to convey information concerning the 'degree zero' (i.e. the tense of the narrative, §3), it conveys recovered information (an antecedent event or flashback) or even a comment on the main events (background).

a. *QATAL in narrative*

§15. At the outset it is important to note that QATAL is always non-initial in narrative. That is to say, it never heads a sentence, in contrast to WAYYIQTOL which always comes first. QATAL, then, is always preceded by something which has first position in the sentence. If it is a conjunction or a particle then we have the 'retrospective' QATAL (§8); if it is a nominal or adverbial element then we have the (WAW-)x-QATAL construction (usually with WAW though it is optional). In narrative, weQATAL can also occur even though it is a comment construction belonging to background (§46).

Now according to the definition given above (§6) the WAW-x-QATAL construction does not comprise a verb clause; it is, instead, a compound noun clause. The information it communicates belongs neither to degree zero nor to the foreground. Depending on where it is in relation to the narrative WAYYIQTOL the WAW-x-QATAL can be: (1) initial, when it precedes the narrative form, (2) non-initial when it follows. In the first case it communicates recovered information (antecedent, §3, 3), in the second, peripheral information (background, §3, 2). The following table will make this difference clear:

(1) initial WAW-x-QATAL = antecedent	(2) non-initial WAW-x-QATAL = background
WAW-x-QATAL = recovered information	WAYYIQTOL = foreground
↓	↓
WAYYIQTOL = degree zero (linguistic perspective, §3, 3)	WAW-x-QATAL = background (prominence, §3, 2)

(1) *Initial WAW-x-QATAL*

§16. The information that Joseph had been taken to Egypt is given in the following terms in Gen. 37.28:

(His brothers sold Joseph to the Ishmaelites)

ויביאו את־יוסף מצרימה

and they brought Joseph down to Egypt

WAYYIQTOL is used to provide the historical information of the event (narrative). The same information appears again, further on in 39.1, in different guise:

ויוסף הורד מרצימה

Now Joseph had been taken down to Egypt

Here this information is not at degree zero of the narrative, unlike 37.28; instead the reader is reminded of it so that he can understand the narrative which follows. Evidently, the information given in 39.1 is no longer narrative (the event has already been described!) but 'recovered information'. QATAL, therefore, is not a narrative form but retrospective, since its function is to introduce the event which comes before the ensuing narrative. It recalls information already given and so resumes the narrative thread which was interrupted by the Judah–Tamar episode (Gen. 38). It is a classic example of the literary 'reprise' (*Wiederaufnahme*, cf. §29, note 30).

Another, very similar example concerns the death of Samuel, narrated in 1 Sam. 25.1 as וימת שמואל. In 1 Sam. 28.3 the same information is not conveyed by WAYYIQTOL but by a QATAL: ושמואל מת 'Now Samuel was dead'. This is no longer narrative but information recalled in order to provide an antecedent to the account which follows (Saul calls up Samuel, who is dead, by means of the necromancer of Endor).

These two examples are enough to show the difference between the two constructions: initial WAW-x-QATAL provides information which precedes the account that follows (retrospective); WAYYIQTOL, instead, is the verb form used for the story itself (degree zero). In the two examples cited the antecedent information had already been given previously in the text. That is why they are particularly suitable for showing the difference between WAW-x-QATAL and WAYYIQTOL. Note, however, that this is not essential. In other words, any information, even new information, can be communicated by an antecedent construction. It is up to the author to decide at which level he should give information of any kind.

§17. It is now clear why the following statement by Joüon (also found in most traditional grammars) needs to be revised 'Usually a narrative begins with qatal (parfait historique) and continues with wayyiqtol. . . But the wayyiqtol has become the narrative tense to such an extent that it is even used at the beginning of a narrative, or at least at a relative beginning'.[20] Four comments can be made here.

1. Narrative never begins with QATAL; initial QATAL only denotes the antecedent;

2. the narrative proper begins with a WAYYIQTOL;

3. Joüon's statement is based on the conviction that by nature WAYYIQTOL is not an initial form but a continuation form. This conviction cannot be discussed at the diachronic level (origin and development of WAYYIQTOL) because we lack the necessary data (§1). But it seems evident to me that the synchronic level (the use of WAYYIQTOL in texts) is the only purely narrative form and is used both as an initial and as a continuation form.

4. Whether WAYYIQTOL is only used for a relative beginning or for the absolute beginning of a narrative or block of narrative[21] cannot be considered here because of the literary-critical implications.[22]

§18. The conclusion reached concerning the form for degree zero, WAYYIQTOL, and the retrospective initial form (WAW-x-QATAL) is important for understanding the syntax of Gen. 1.1-3, a text which has been much discussed although no commonly accepted solution has been reached.[23]

Gen. 1

| 1 (a) | בראשית ברא אלהים את השמים ואת הארץ |
| 2 (b) | והארץ היתה תהו ובהו |

(c)   וחשך על־פני תהום
(d)   ורוח אלהים מרחפת על־פני המים
3   ויאמר אלהים. . .

The grammatical analysis of the four sentences in vv. 1-2 is as
follows: (a) x-QATAL, (b) WAW-x-QATAL, (c) WAW-simple noun
clause (noun + prepositional phrase), (d) WAW-simple noun clause
(noun + participle). In view of what has already been said (§§16-17),
then vv. 1-2 comprise the antecedent and v. 3 is the beginning of the
actual narrative.

It is more difficult to determine the relationship between v. 1 and
v. 2. Personally, I think v. 1 is a temporal clause. The expression
בראשית ברא אלהים should, in fact, be understood as in the construct
state with a finite verb as the 'nomen rectum':[24] 'At the beginning of
God-created. . .', in other words, 'When God began to create. . .' I
also think that vv. 1-2 comprise an independent clause as is the case
when other narratives are introduced by 'antecedent' phrases (cf.
§19). Accordingly, v. 1 (temporal phrase) functions as the 'protasis'
while v. 2 is the 'apodosis' (the terms 'protasis' and 'apodosis' are
used broadly here, cf. §96). The translation then is

1   When God began to create the heavens and the earth,
2   the earth was formless and empty,
      darkness was above the abyss
      and the spirit of God was hovering over the waters.
3   Then God said. . .

In vv. 1-2, then, we have four 'retrospective' forms (or forms
denoting the antecedent), all noun clauses (the first two, compound,
the other two simple). In terms of syntax, clauses (a) and (b)
comprise the protasis (x-QATAL) and the apodosis (WAW-x-
QATAL); this means they are linked as in the 'two-element syntactic
pattern' (§105). Clauses (c) and (d) are co-ordinate with (b) and
communicate contemporaneous data. All four clauses together
comprise the antecedent to the narrative proper, which begins with a
WAYYIQTOL.[25]

§19. This syntactic pattern (antecedent—beginning of narrative) is
not confined to the first verses of Gen. 1; it often occurs in the OT.
For example, in the first four chapters of Genesis:

Gen. 2.5-6[6] (antecedent)

5   וכל שיח השדה טרם יהיה בארץ
                  וכל־עשב השדה טרם יצמח
           כי לא המטיר יהוה אלהים על־הארץ
              ואדם אין לעבד את־האדמה
6   ואד יעלה מן־הארץ
               והשקה את־כל־פני־האדמה

+ 2.7 (beginning of the narrative)

                  . . . וייצר יהוה אלהים את־האדם

5 Now no bush of the field yet existed on the earth,
    and no grass of the field had yet sprouted,
    for Y. had not yet sent rain upon the earth
    and there was no man to till the earth.
6 A flow(?) rose up from the earth
    and watered the whole surface of the earth.
7 Then Y. formed man. . .

Gen. 2.10-14

10   ונהר יצא מעדן להשקות את־הגן
                        ומשם יפרד
                    והיה לארבעה ראשים
. . . (vv. 11-14: names of the four rivers and each of their
      regions, using simple nominal clauses)

+ 2.15 (beginning of the narrative)

                  . . . ויקח יהוה אלהים את־האדם

10 Now a river came out from Eden to water the garden,
    and from there it was divided up
    and became four streams. .

15 Then Y. took Man. . . .

Gen. 3.1a (antecedent)

     והנחש היה ערום מכל חית השדה אשר עשה יהוה אלהים

+ 3.1b

                      . . . ויאמר אל־האשה

Now the serpent was the most cunning of all the animals of the
    field which Y. God had made
He said to the woman

Gen. 4.1a (antecedent)

והאדם ידע את־חוה אשתו

+ 4.1b (beginning of the narrative)

ותהר . . .

Now Adam knew Eve, his wife.
She conceived. . .

We can conclude by listing the following 'constructions with antecedent':

  (i)   WAW-x-QATAL for a single action (presented as) occurring
        once in the past (3.1a; 4.1a);
 (ii)   WAW-x-YIQTOL (continued by a weQATAL) for a repeated
        past action (2.6);
(iii)   WAW-simple nominal clause with participle (equivalent to a
        WAW-x-YIQTOL construction, which besides weQATAL is
        the attested continuation form) (2.10) for a repeated past
        action.

In both WAW-x-טרם-YIQTOL constructions (2.5) the choice of YIQTOL is conditioned by the presence of the conjunction טרם, 'not yet' (§171).

Recognition of this syntactic pattern, here and elsewhere, is important in order to separate the different levels of narrative: the 'retrospective' level (complex or simple noun clause) by which the author provides the prelude to the narrative, and the level of degree zero (WAYYIQTOL) which begins the narrative proper.

Note that each of the various 'retrospective' constructions comprises a clause which is grammatically independent but syntactically is dependent (§126.5)

§20. In addition it should be noted that the initial WAW-x-QATAL construction also occurs within a narrative. In this case, even though not initial in the absolute meaning of the term, it fulfils an analogous function. In effect, the narrative flow is broken to provide information required for the continuation of the actual narrative (cf. §40, interruption of the WAYYIQTOL-chain to formulate a prior circumstance and §45 to denote a circumstance which belongs to the following WAYYIQTOL). On the textual function of antecedent constructions (contrasted with those using *wayehi*) see §36.

(2) *non-initial (WAW-)x-QATAL*

§21. When preceded by an element which is nominal (noun) or adverbial (preposition + noun, true adverb), with or without WAW, the QATAL is used to provide comment on an aspect of the preceding main action, expressed by WAYYIQTOL, or to portray another action against the background of the first (§9). For more detail cf. §§41-42, 48.

b. *QATAL in discourse*

§22. A very important fact concerning the use of QATAL in discourse is that it always comes first in the sentence; this never occurs in narrative.

Polotsky[28] identified a special use of QATAL in discourse which we can term the 'QATAL for reporting'. He cites two examples in the bible where a QATAL is contrasted with a YIQTOL with reference to the same event. When the event is related in 'narrative' the WAYYIQTOL is used; but when the same event is reported in 'discourse', after verbs of 'saying', 'telling', 'hearing' ('report'), QATAL is used. The two examples cited by Polotsky are

2 Sam. 12.26-27

26	וילחם יואב ברבת בני עמון
	וילכד את־עיר המלוכה
27	וישלח יואב מלאכים אל־דוד ויאמר
	נלחמתי ברבה
	גם־לכדתי את־עיר המים

26   Joab waged war against Rabbah of the Ammonites and captured the royal city.

27   Then Joab sent ambassadors to David to say:
'I waged war against Rabbah
and I also captured the city of waters'.

1 Kgs 16.9–10.16

9	ויקשר עליו עבדו זמרי שר מחצית הרכב ...
10	ויבא זמרי ויכהו וימיתהו ...
16	וישמע העם החנים לאמר
	קשר זמרי
	וגם הכה המלך

9   His servant, Zimri, chief of half the chariot-contingent, conspired against him (the king of Elam)...

10   Zimri arrived, struck him and killed him...

16   The people who were encamped heard tell:
           'Zimri made a conspiracy
           and also struck the king'.

These two examples show clearly how the same event can be
described using the same terms but with different verbal forms:
WAYYIQTOL in 'narrative' ('Erzählung'), QATAL in 'report'
('Rede' or 'Bericht'). Note that in English, as in other European
languages, WAYYIQTOL corresponds to the simple past while
QATAL is rendered by the present perfect, a tense which belongs to
the 'realm of comment'. This fact is further proof that QATAL is not
a 'narrative' verbal form (§14).

§23. Once this opposition (WAYYIQTOL vs QATAL) has been
identified it is not hard to find other examples:

Gen. 40.2

ויקצף פרעה 'Pharaoh was angry' (narrative)
vs 41.10 (the chief butler is speaking): פרעה קצף (discourse);

Gen. 40.5

ויחלמו חלום שניהם 'And they both had a dream'
vs 40.8 (both of Pharaoh's officers are speaking): חלום חלמנו;

Gen. 40.21

וישב את־שר המשקים 'And he (Pharaoh) reinstated the chief
           butler'
vs 41.13b (the chief butler is speaking): אתי השיב;

Gen. 42.7

וידבר אתם קשות 'And he (Joseph) spoke harshly with them'
vs 42.30 (the brothers are reporting to Jacob):
דבר האיש... אתנו קשות;

Gen. 46.6

ויבאו מצרימה 'And they (Jacob and his sons) came to Egypt'
vs 47.1 (Joseph is reporting to Pharaoh)
אבי ואחי באו ... מארץ כנען (cf. v. 5);

Deut. 5.28a

וישמע יהוה את־קול דבריכם 'And Yahweh heard (the sound of) your
           words' (Moses is speaking)
vs 5.28b (Yahweh to Moses) שמעתי את־קול דברי העם;

2 Sam. 3.20

ויבא אבנר אל־דוד 'And Abner came to David'
vs 3.23 (as reported to Joab): בא־אבנר בן־נר אל־המלך;

2 Sam. 6.11b

ויברך יהוה את־עבד אדם ואת־כל־ביתו 'And Yahweh blessed Obed-
Edom and all his household'
vs 6.12a (as reported to King David): ברך יהוה את־בית עבד אדם;

1 Kgs 20.17a

ויצאו נערי שרי המדינות 'And out sallied the young men of the
provincial governors'
vs 20.17b (as reported to Ben-Hadad): אנשים יצאו משמרון.

Further examples are: Exod. 18.5 vs 18.6; Judg. 14.1 vs 14.2; 16.1 vs
16.2; 1 Sam. 4.10 vs 4.17; 1 Kgs 1.50 vs 1.51; 21.13 vs 21.14; 2 Kgs 3.5
vs 3.7; 7.5 vs 7.10; 2 Chron. 12.6 vs 12.7.

Two concluding comments can be made:

(1) the 'report' QATAL never heads a sentence but can be preceded
by a particle (גם or וגם in 2 Sam. 12.27 and 1 Kgs 16.16), by the
subject (Gen. 41.10; 47.1; 1 Kgs 20.17) or by the object (Gen. 40.8;
41.13). In these cases we have the x-QATAL construction for reports
(cf. §77).

(2) The same opposition WAYYIQTOL vs QATAL is found in
narrative discourse (Deut 5.28; cf. §74 for the terminology). Note,
finally, that from the syntactic aspect the 'report' QATAL differs
from retrospective QATAL in two ways: it is a form with first
position in the clause and it is at degree zero (cf. §135, no. 3).

§24. It must be stressed that the use of QATAL described in the two
preceding paragraphs is intrinsically linked with the setting as
'report', the announcement of information which the addressee does
not yet know. What happens is that when known events are reported
the verb form used is WAYYIQTOL, not QATAL, and the passage is
no longer a 'report' but a 'narrative discourse' (§74). This will be
clearly shown in the examples that follow.

Num. 20

14 (Message from Moses to the King of Edom):
אתה ידעת את כל־התלאה אשר מצאתנו
15 וירדו אבתינו מצרימה . . .

14 You know all the tribulations which we have encountered.
15 Our Fathers went down to Egypt. . .

Deut. 29

15 (Moses' speech to the people):
כי־אתם ידעתם את אשר־ישבנו בארץ מצרים . . .
16
ותראו את־השקוציהם . . .
15 For you know that we used to live in the land of Egypt. . .
16 You have seen their abominations. . .

2 Chron. 13

Abijah king of Judah said to Jeroboam and all Israel):
5
הלא לכם לדעת כי יהוה אלהי ישראל נתן ממלכה לדויד . . .
6
ויקם ירבעם . . .
5 Is it not your duty to know that Y., God of Israel, has given a
kingdom to David. . .?
6 But up rose Jeroboam. . .

A different type of 'report' is used when an event is related which is
taking place the same time as the message, for example:

2 Sam. 19.2

ויגד ליואב
הנה המלך בכה
ויתאבל על־אבשלם

And Joab was told:
(etc., §68).

It is important to note that in all the examples given, WAYYIQTOL
never comes first in speech; the exact opposite is true of narrative. It
is always preceded by a construction typical of discourse: x-QATAL
in Num. 20.14 and Deut. 29.15, an interrogative sentence in 2 Chron.
13.5, a simple nominal clause in 2 Sam. 19.2. We can therefore
summarize the relationship between WAYYIQTOL and QATAL on
the basis of their position in narrative and in discourse as follows:

	Narrative	Discourse
WAYYIQTOL	1st position	2nd position
QATAL	2nd position	1st position

§25. Besides its use in the 'report' (§§22-23), QATAL in discourse
has retrospective force as in narrative (§8).[29] In view of the word

order (§134) it is the function of the x (circumstance/subject)-
QATAL construction to place the emphasis on the element 'x', as is
also true of prose (§48).

Gen. 42.9

ויאמר אלהם
מרגלים אתם
לראות את־ערות הארץ באתם

And (Joseph) said to them (his brothers):
'You are spies;
it is to see the nakedness of the land that you have
come!'

In 42.12, instead, this becomes לא כי־ערות הארץ באתם לראות 'No, but
you have come in order to see the nakedness of the land'.

Gen. 47.4

לגור בארץ באנו

(Joseph's brothers say to Pharaoh): It is in order to reside as
'guests' in the land that we have come.

2 Kgs 18.25 (cf. Isa. 38.10)

עתה המבלעדי יהוה עליתי על המקום הזה להשחתו
יהוה אמר אלי עלה

So, is it perhaps against Yahweh's will that I have come up against
this place in order to destroy it?
And Y told me: 'Go up!'

Chapter 5

HEBREW NARRATIVE

§26. Narrative can begin straight off with a WAYYIQTOL. However, when a circumstance or another nominal element comes before the principal action, this action is expressed by QATAL. Compare 1 Kgs 11.42:

והימים אשר מלך שלמה. . .ארבעים שנה

Now the time ('the days') that Solomon reigned. . . . were 40 years,

with the parallel 2 Chron. 9.30:

וימלך שלמה. . .ארבעים שנה

similarly 1 Kgs 15.17 (without the date):

ויעל בעשא

with the parallel 2 Chron. 16.1 (with the date before the verb):

בשנת. . .עלה בעשא

In the year. . . Baasha went up;

and also 2 Kgs 18.17 (= Isa. 36.2):

וישלח מלך־אשור

with the parallel 2 Chron. 32.9:

אחר זה שלח סנחריב מלך־אשור

After this, Sennacherib, king of Assyria, sent. . .

Instances of a narrative opening with a circumstance affecting the main action are quite common. In the following paragraphs we will examine the most frequently occurring constructions of this type. Other cases of the same kind are considered below under the heading 'the two-element syntactic construction' (§§96ff.).

a. *The beginning of a narrative*

(1) WAW-x-QATAL

§27. As has been seen (§16) the WAW-x-QATAL construction provides recovered information which has to function as a prelude to the narrative which follows. Sometimes, instead of being very brief such information develops into a 'short independent narrative',[30] though retaining its function as prelude to the narrative proper.

1 Sam. 28.3

ושמואל מת
ויספדו־לו כל־ישראל
ויקברהו ברמה ובעירו
ושאול הסיר האבות ואת־הידעונים מהארץ

> Now Samuel was dead,
> > and all Israel had mourned him
> > and had buried him in Ramah, that is in his city.
> Now Saul had removed the necromancers and the diviners from
> > the land.

The text clearly provides two items of recovered information which form the prelude to the narrative: 'Now Samuel was dead. . . '; 'Now Saul had removed . . .'; both are signalled by WAW-x-QATAL. The first item of information, however, is embellished by details concerning the lament for Samuel and his burial. These particulars are expressed by two WAYYIQTOLs and so comprise a short narrative which still belongs to the prelude. Note that in this case the two WAYYIQTOLs are non-initial and are in the same tense (the pluperfect) as the retrospective WAW-x-QATAL construction, of which they are the continuation. This is an exception due to the syntactic link with the retrospective construction (cf. §40). The actual narrative begins with WAYYIQTOL in v. 4.

(2) *wayehi*[31]

§28. *wayehi* is the supreme 'macro-syntactic sign' of narrative (§12). This means that its presence is enough to mark the passage as narrative, though not necessarily a narrative which is historical and detached (even though by the far the most common type) but also reported narrative or 'narrative discourse' (for example, Gen. 44.24, §78). The textual function of *wayehi* is to introduce a new element into the main narrative thread so that that element becomes an integral and important part of the account (§36). For an appraisal of the syntactic character of *wayehi* see §127.2. Examination of two passages will provide a useful introduction to the topic.

Judg. 11

1 ויפתח הגלעדי היה גבור חיל
והוא בן־אשה זונה
ויולד גלעד את־יפתח
2 ותלד אשת־גלעד לו בנים
ויגדלו בני־האשה
ויגרשו את־יפתח ויאמרו לו
(direct speech follows)
3 ויברח יפתח מפני אחיו
וישב בארץ טוב
ויתלקטו אל־יפתח אנשים ריקים
ויצאו עמו

1 Now Jephthah the Gileadite was a doughty warrior
  but he was a prostitute's son
  and Gilead had sired Jephthah.
2 Now Gilead's wife gave birth to his sons
  and the sons of the wife grew up.
  Then they ousted Jephthah and said to him
  (direct speech follows)
3 And Jephthah fled from his brothers
  and lived in the Land of Tob.
  And drifters gathered round Jephthah
  and went with him on raids.

The initial circumstance, expressed by the WAW-x-QATAL construction, becomes a short self-contained story, developed by a series of WAYYIQTOLs which continue the opening construction (cf. §27); accordingly, this story belongs to the prelude (vv. 1-3). The narrative, interrupted by this antecedent, is taken up again in v. 4 by *wayehi*. It recalls information already mentioned in 10.17—the mobilization of the Ammonites—and brings the text of the antecedent event into the narrative. In v. 5 another *wayehi* appears which introduces the protagonist, Jephthah, in the context of the war. Accordingly, the two *wayehi*'s mark off the passage as narrative and at the same time indicate the two basic components of the account: the war and Jephthah's role in it.

Note that in both cases a circumstantial construction follows the *wayehi*:

v. 4

ויהי מימים

וילחמו בני־עמן עם־ישראל

After a certain period

the Ammonites waged war on Israel.

v. 5

ויהי כאשר־נלחמו בני־עמן עם־ישראל

וילכו זקני גלעד לקחת את־יפתח מארץ טוב

When the Ammonites actually waged war against Israel, the elders of Gilead went to collect Jephthah from the land of Tob.

§29. 1 Sam. 30

1

ויהי כבא דוד ואנשיו צקלג ביום השלישי

ועמלקי (ketib) פשטו אל־נגב ואל־צקלג

ויכו את־צקלג

וישרפו אתה באש

2

וישבו את־הנשים אשר־בה

מקטן ועד־גדול לא המיתו איש

וינהגו

וילכו לדרכם

3

ויבא דוד ואנשיו אל־העיר

והנה שרופה באש

ונשיהם ובניהם ובנתיהם נשבו

1 When David and his men reached Ziglag on the third day
   (the situation was as follows):
        The Amalekites had raided the Negeb and Ziglag.
        They had attacked Ziglag
        and they had burned it with fire

2   they had taken captive the women who were in it:
        from the youngest to the oldest they had killed no-one,
        but had led them away
        and they had gone their way.

3 So David and his men reached the city,
        and behold: it had been burnt with fire
        and their wives, their sons and their daughters had been taken
                prisoner.

In this passage, too, *wayehi* introduces a temporal circumstance ('protasis') to which is connected the WAW-x-QATAL construction ('apodosis'). In its turn this construction develops into a short self-contained story described in a series of WAYYIQTOLs (§27), interrupted only in v. 2 by the negative x-QATAL construction in order to place the emphasis on the 'rider' 'from the youngest to the oldest'[32] which comes before the verb (cf. §48). From v. 3 it is evident that the WAW-x-QATAL construction ועמלקי פשטו and the short account which follows (vv. 1-2) form the prelude to the following narrative: everything happens before David's arrival. The WAW-x-QATAL, therefore, is a retrospective construction and the passage is set in the past perfect. In fact, the narrative mentions the arrival of David and his men at Ziglag (with *wayehi*), then pauses to relate what had happened previously (with an antecedent construction), and finally resumes the initial information (using WAYYIQTOL) adding that David and his men saw for themselves (*wehinneh*) what had happened. Verse 3 comprises a literary reprise (*Wiederaufnahme*) of v. 1; that is why I translate 'So (David and his men) reached (the city). . . '.[33] The narrative does not really start until v. 4.

Note, in v. 1, the quite rare example of an antecedent construction ואמלקי פשטו which occurs in the 'apodosis' after a circumstantial clause of time introduced by *wayehi* and comprises an independent clause, like other corresponding constructions (§19). Another example of this kind is:

2 Sam. 13.1

ויהי אחרי־כן

ולאבשלום בן־דוד אחות יפה

Now, after this.
(the reader should know that) Absalom, David's son, had a beautiful sister.

An analogous example occurs in the apodosis of the 'two-member syntactic construction' (Exod. 10.13b, §105): here the antecedent construction corresponds to the pluperfect.

§30. As is evident by now from the examples studied, *wayehi* has the function of introducing a temporal clause which must come before the main action. A temporal circumstance, whether precise or generic, can be expressed by the following constructions:[34]

Type (a)	adverb of time or prep. + noun
Type (b)	prep. + inf.
Type (c)	כאשר/כי (etc.) + finite verb, or a participle functioning as a conditional, or a conditional relative clause
Type (d)	a simple or compound nominal clause

When two temporal circumstances are expressed, the *wayehi* introducing the first generally applies to the second as well (cf. 2 Kgs 3.20, §33; 2 Chron. 24.11, §35. Sometimes, though, the *wayehi* is repeated:

Exod. 12.41

ויהי מקץ שלשים שנה וארבע מאות שנה
ויהי בעצם היום הזה
יצאו כל־צבאות יהוה מארץ מצרים

So, after 430 years,
on exactly this day
all the tribes of Y. left the land of Egypt.

Note, however, that in the following example, the function of each *wayehi* is different. The first is a 'macro-syntactic sign' of the narrative we are examining while the second—which is a 'full' verb (§§36, 127)—comprises the 'apodosis':

2 Sam. 7.4

ויהי בלילה ההוא
ויהי דבר־יהוה אל־נתן לאמר

But that night
the word of Yahweh came to Nathan as follows.

§31. The principal action (the 'apodosis'), which comes after the temporal circumstance, is expressed by the following constructions:
(i) WAYYIQTOL,[35] for a single past action

Gen. 40.20

(temporal circumstance, type a)   ויהי ביום השלישי ...
ויעש משתה לכל־עבדיו

Indeed, on the third day... he (Pharaoh) made a feast for all his servants.

§32. (ii) QATAL, or WAW-x-QATAL,[36] for a single past action.
(a) The subject comes after QATAL (QATAL-x) but occasionally precedes it (x-QATAL).
2 Kgs 18.1

(type a) ... ויהי בשנת
... מלך חזקיה

In the year... Hezekiah began to reign...

1 Kgs 11.4

ויהי לעת זקנת שלמה (type a)
נשיו הטו את־לבבו אחרי אלהים אחרים

Accordingly, at the time of Solomon's old age
his wives turned his heart towards strange gods

When the subject remains the same it does not have to be repeated in
the 'apodosis'.

1 Kgs 8.54

ויהי ככלות שלמה להתפלל ...(type b)
קם מלפני מזבח יהוה

As soon as Solomon finished praying
he got up from in front of the altar of Yahweh.

2 Kgs 13.21

ויהי הם קברים איש (type d)
והנה ראו את־הגדוד

On one occasion, while they were burying a man,
suddenly, they saw the band (of marauding Moabites).

1 Kgs 16.11

ויהי במלכו כשבתו על־כסאו (type b, twice)
הכה את־כל־בית בעשא

Now when he began to reign, as soon as he sat on the throne
(Zimri) murdered all the house of Baasha.

We can remark in passing that, on the basis of this text, *be* + infinitive
generally denotes simultaneity of action while *ke* + infinitive
emphasizes that an action follows immediately.

(b) QATAL sometimes occurs in the construction WAW(- *hinneh*/
הנה)-x (Subject)-QATAL.

2 Sam. 13.30

ויהי המה בדרך (type d)
והשמעה באה אל־דוד

But while they were still on the way
the news reached David.

2 Kgs 20.4

ויהי ישעיהו לא יצא העיר התכנה (type d)
ודבר־יהוה היה אליו

When Isaiah had not yet emerged from the inner city
the word of Y. came to him.

2 Sam. 13.36

ויהי ככלתו לדבר (type b)
והנה בני־המלך באו

And as soon as he (Jonadab) had finished speaking
the king's sons came...

For discussion of the function of these constructions (QATAL and
[WAW-] complex noun clause) cf. §127.

§33. (iii) Simple nominal clause, for a contemporaneous action

Gen. 24.15

ויהי־הוא טרם כלה לדבר (type d)
והנה רבקה יצאת

Before he had even finished speaking
Rebecca came out.

Gen. 42.35

ויהי הם מריקים שקיהם (type d)
והנה־איש צרור־כספו בשקו

But while they were emptying their sacks
everyone's purse of money ('each, the purse of his money') was in
his own sack.

2 Kgs 3.20

ויהי בבקר (type a)
כעלות המנחה (type b)
והנה־מים באים מדרך אדום

And indeed in the morning
while sacrifice was being offered
water was coming from the direction of Edom.

§34. (iv) YIQTOL or weQATAL ('inverted form'), for a repeated
action[37]

1 Kgs 14.28

ויהי מדי־בא המלך בית יהוה (type b)
ישאום הרצים

And every time the king went to the temple of Yahweh
the guards took them (the shields).

2 Kgs 4.8b

ויהי מדי עברו

יסר שמה לאכל־לחם

And so every time he (Elisha) passed that way
he would turn in there (the Sunamite woman's house) to eat.

§35. The use of weQATAL for a repeated action is clearly shown in the following example.

2 Chron. 24.11

ויהי בעת יביא את־הארון אל־פקדת המלך ביד הלוים (type c)

וכראותם כי־רב הכסף (type b)

ובא סופר המלך ופקיד כהן הראש

ויערו את־הארון

וישאהו

וישיבהו אל־מקמו

כה עשו ליום ביום

And the moment they brought the cash-box for the king's
      inspection at the hands of the Levites,
as soon as they saw that the money was plentiful
along came the royal scribe and the high priest's inspector,
(?)emptied the cash-box
hoisted it up
and put it back in its place.
They did this day after day.

The repeated action is expressed by weQATAL (ובא ספר ...). The YIQTOL which comes after the *wayehi* (בעת יבא) shows that the action is repeated. However, the three weYIQTOL's which follow the weQATAL are difficult to explain. The fact is that in classical Hebrew weYIQTOL is used as the indirect jussive (§§61-64) and not as a continuation form of weQATAL (§55.1). That is why I inserted a question mark in the translation, above. A translation corresponding to the normal use of weYIQTOL would be as follows: 'they came... in order to empty..., to hoist it up and to put it back'.

2 Kgs 12.10b-12, has a different structure:

10b   בבוא־איש בית יהוה (type b but minus the *wayehi*)

ונתנו־שמה הכהנים שמרי הסף את־כל־הכסף המובא בית־יהוה

11   ויהי כראותם כי־רב הכסף בארון (type b)

ויעל ספר המלך והכהן הגדול

ויצרו

וימנו את־הכסף הנמצא בית־יהוה

12   ...ונתנו את־הכסף המתכן על־ידי עשי המלאכה

10b When someone came to the temple of Yahweh.
    there (in the cash-box) the priests guarding the threshold
    placed all the money that was brought to Yahweh's temple.
11 Accordingly, as soon as they saw that the money in the cash-
    box was plentiful
    up would go a royal scribe and the high priest,
    they would ??
    they would count the money that was found in the temple of
    Yahweh.
12 and would place the checked money in the hands of the
    workmen...

The passage begins (v. 10b) and ends (v. 12) with a weQATAL (ונתנו)
expressing a repeated action even though the antecedent circumstance
is not introduced by *wayehi* (cf. 'the two-member syntactic construction',
§113.3). This shows that the four intervening WAYYQITOLs are not
narrative WAYYIQTOLs but a continuation the weQATAL and so
have the same tense as the repeated action in the past (cf. the
comparable 'phenonemon' of 'narrative comment', §84, and §146 for
the 'continuation' WAYYIQTOL). 2 Kgs 12.10b-12, therefore,
conveys the same meaning as 2 Chron. 24.11 but uses slightly
different grammatical forms.

§36. Since all the constructions listed above (§§28-35) also occur
without *wayehi* (§§37-38, 112) it follows that it is an important but
optional signal within narrative. From syntactic analysis (§127) it is
clear that *wayehi* has no function at all in respect of the single clause
which follows as it makes no difference of any kind to its syntactic
structure. At most it shows that the following circumstance (or
name) is a 'casus pendens' (§124). Even if it has no syntactic function
this does not imply that it is of no use in the text. Its function, rather,
is determined by text linguistics and is to be found in longer narrative
units than the individual sentence. What is here termed a 'narrative
unit' corresponds to Weinrich's 'text'. 'A text is a logical (i.e.
intelligible and consistent) sequence of linguistic signs, placed
between two significant breaks in communication'.[8]

Now in the narrative unit, in Hebrew, two types of 'significant
breaks in communication' can be listed. The first is the historical
date-formula (§37), the other comprises the various constructions for
antecedents (§§16-20).

In the books of Kings the date-formula is often used to introduce the deeds of the individual kings of Judah or Israel. For example: 1 Kgs 15.1 (Abijam); 15.9 (Asa); 15.33 (Ba'asha); 16.8 (Elah); 16.15 (Zimri); 16.23 (Omri); etc. It is quite evident, then, that it marks off a narrative unit which can be of varying length.

The antecedent constructions serve the same purpose, coming as they must at the beginning of a narrative (or of part of a narrative) and preceding the narrative proper (WAYYIQTOL) and they provide the information required to understand the actual narrative. It follows that a narrative unit is often marked off both by the antecedent event which introduces it and by the antecedent to the following narrative.

It is important to note that when used for 'significant breaks in communication', neither the date-formula nor the antecedent constructions are preceded by *wayehi*. In contrast it is reasonable to conclude from this that *wayehi* has the opposite function: to connect the circumstance which follows it with the main narrative thread. In other words, it avoids a break in communication. We can verify this hypothesis by examining Exodus 1–4 from the aspect of text linguistics.

(a) Chapters 1–2 comprise a narrative unit sandwiched between the initial antecedent (1.1-7) and the antecedent of the following unit (3.1).

- A *wayehi* occurs in 1.5, but it is a WAYYIQTOL of the 'full' verb (not the macro-syntactic marker for narrative) and its function is closural: 'And so they were. . . ' (cf. §38, note 36). It belongs, therefore, to the antecedent as do the following clauses with which it is connected. Remember that in vv. 5-7 a double tense shift of the type WAYYIQTOL → WAW-x-QATAL (§9) occurs.
- The actual narrative (degree zero) begins with the WAYYIQTOL of v. 8 and continues with a chain of this same narrative form.
- In 1.21 the function of the *wayehi* is to connect the circumstance ('since the midwives revered God') with the preceding line of narrative of degree zero, resuming v. 17. The *wayehi* of 2.11 has the same function, where the circumstance is 'in those days' and the same applies to 2.23 where the *wayehi* connects with the circumstance 'after many days'.

— In 2.16 we have an antecedent construction: ולכהן מדין שבע בנות, 'Now the priest of Midian had seven daughters'. From the context, however, it is clear that this is not 'a significant break in communication' but a slight pause, since the narrative then returns to the same topic.

(b) Chapters 3–4 comprise a second narrative unit introduced by an antecedent construction: ומשה היה רעה את־צאן יתרו כהן מדין, 'Now Moses was pasturing the flock of Jethro, priest of Midian' (3.1). This syntactic break is 'significant' because it marks the beginning of a new topic (the call of Moses).

— The narrative flows uninterruptedly in a chain of WAYYIQTOLs which also joins together several passages in direct speech.
— The *wayehi* of 4.24 functions as a connector between the circumstance ('on the road, in the khan') and the main line of narrative.

(c) From the criteria adopted in the present analysis chapters 5-14 form a lengthy narrative unit because they come between two antecedent constructions: 5.1 ואחר באו משה ואהרן ויאמרו אל־פרעה, 'Now after this Moses and Aaron went to say ('and said') to the pharaoh'; and 15.1 אז ישיר־משה ובני ישראל את־השירה הזאת ליהוה, 'Then Moses and the Israelites sang this song for Y'. Note that both these two constructions (5.1 and 15.1) are complex nominal clauses, the first using QATAL, the second using YIQTOL for reasons of grammar (for the presence of אז, cf. §171). Chapters 5-14 form a single narrative unit, as is shown by the criterion of location: from 5.1 on the events take place in Egypt right up to the departure from Egypt; after 15.1 the various stages of passage through the desert begin (with a series of WAYYIQTOLs with the root נסע, 'to leave'; for example, 15.22: ויסע; 16.1 ויסעו; 17.1 ויסעו; etc.). Within this large narrative unit there are no 'significant breaks in communication'. In order to identify the smaller subdivisions, therefore, other criteria (literary, exegetical, etc.) have to be adopted.

— In 6.14-27 the narrative is interrupted by a list of the names of the clan chiefs in order to determine the ancestors of the protagonists, Moses and Aaron. This interruption is unimportant, though, as it is framed by a literary inclusio.

The *wayehi* of 6.28 introduces a circumstance ('on the day Y. spoke to Moses in the land of Egypt') which is a resumption of 6.13 ('Y. spoke to Moses... from the land of Egypt').

— In 10.13b there is another minor interruption of the main narrative thread: הבקר היה 'When it was morning', a complex nominal clause with the function of protasis in a 'two-member syntactic construction' (§105).

— The *wayehi* of 12.29 connects the circumstance ('at midnight') with the main narrative thread and at the same time alludes to the divine promise of 11.4-5 (plague of the first-born) to describe its fulfilment, after the interruption concerning the Passover.

— The *wayehi* of 12.41 (with closural force: 'And so, after 430 years...') brings the foregoing antecedent construction (12.40 'Now the period the Israelites lived... was 430 years') back to the main narrative thread.

— Another *wayehi* in 12.51 recalls a circumstance already mentioned in 12.41 ('on that very day') and so includes the instruction concerning the Passover (12.43-50) within the main narrative.

— The *wayehi* of 13.17 introduces a circumstance ('when the Pharaoh allowed the people to leave'). In this way the narrative is resumed after the instruction concerning the first-born (13.1-16).

— In 14.10 an antecedent construction is a momentary interruption to the narrative sequence: ופרעה הקריב 'Now the Pharaoh approached'; but it is immediately resumed again.

— Finally, the *wayehi* of 14.24 connects the circumstance ('in the morning watch') with the main narrative.

From this analysis three conclusions can be drawn. First, the various constructions of antecedent always mark an interruption to the main narrative, but not always a 'significant break'. Each case has to be judged on its own merits from literary criteria and the meaning of the text. Second, in contrast with the antecedent constructions, *wayehi* always effects a connection within the narrative unit. It is required when a circumstance placed prior to the main verb has to be linked with the main narrative thread (degree zero). In more precise terms *wayehi* links the main narrative not just to the individual circumstance of time but also to the whole event it initiates. The *wayehi* also links up the minor subdivisions which are often totally unrelated (such as the instructions concerning the passover and the firstborn in the text analysed above), which would otherwise remain disconnected from the main story. It has the essential function of strengthening quite considerably the 'textuality' (i.e. the inner cohesion and indivisibility) of the text (cf. §79). This connective microsyntactic function accrues to the *wayehi* from its nature as a WAYYIQTOL.

The third important comment is that *wayehi* never occurs at the beginning of an independent narrative unit. In this guise it is clearly distinct from the *wayehi* which is a 'full' form of the verb היה. The latter can, in fact, occur at the absolute beginning of an independent narrative unit, as in Judg. 13.2 (beginning of the story of Sampson); 17.1 (beginning of the story of Micah); 17.7 (beginning of the story about the levite of Bethlehem): 1 Sam. 1.1 (absolute beginning); 9.1 (beginning of the story of Cis). The *wayehi* which is a 'full' verb, therefore, behaves like a normal narrative WAYYIQTOL (§8). Instead, the *wayehi* which is a microsyntactic marker can come at the beginning of a narrative only if it has been introduced by an antecedent. A clear example is Job 1.6 (beginning of the actual narrative after the antecedent of vv. 1-5, §90). The difference is that unlike the *wayehi* of the full verb (narrative WAYYIQTOL) it comes at the absolute beginning of a narrative (without an antecedent). This syntactic peculiarity of *wayehi* will be evaluated in §127.

(3) 'Temporal circumstance' not preceded by *wayehi* (historical date)

§37. A conditional clause of time, expressed by the construction preposition + noun ('year', 'day') (cf. §30, type a) can introduce a narrative even if not preceded by *wayehi*. This happens chiefly in the date-formulas of the books of Kings and Chronicles. The main action is generally expressed by QATAL-subject, but WAYYIQTOL also occurs.

1 Kgs 15.1

ובשנת ...
... מלך אבים

The parallel in 2 Chron. 13.1 has instead:

בשנת ...
ויִמלך אביה

In the year (number)
(name of king) ruled

Isa. 6.1

בשנת ...
ואראה את־אדני

In the year...
I saw Y.

but in Isa. 14.28

בשנת ...
היה המשא הזה

In the year...
came the following oracle.

§38. It is hard to say what the difference is between these constructions and those we have already seen which are identical except for the extra initial *wayehi*.

Often there seems to be absolutely no difference as in 2 Kgs 18.13

ובארבע עשרה שנה למלך חזקיהו
עלה סנחריב מלך־אשור על כל־ערי יהודה הבצרות

In the 14th year of King Hezekiah, Sennacherib, King of Assyria mounted an expedition against all the fortified cities of Judah;

as compared with Isa. 36.1 where *wayehi* is inserted at the beginning of the same formulation. See also 2 Chron. 24.11 and the parallel passage, 2 Kgs 12.10b, cited above (§35).

However, some cases show that the construction with *wayehi* is simply 'narrative' whereas without *wayehi* it is 'commentary' or 'emphatic' (§134), meaning that emphasis is placed on the initial circumstance and so comprises a complex noun clause (cf. §124.2).

1 Kgs 6.1

ויהי בשמונים שנה ...
ויבן הבית ליהוה

In the year (480 from the Exodus...) (Solomon) built the temple of Yahweh.

Instead 1 Kgs 6

37   בשנה הרביעית יֻסַּד בית יהוה בירח זו

38   ...כְּלָה הבית... ובשנה האחת עשרה בירח בול

                          ויבנהו שבע שנים

37   In the fourth year the foundations of the Temple of Yahweh
      were laid, in the month of Ziv/ 38 the 11th year, in the month of
      Bul . . . he completed the Temple.
      And so he built it in 7 years.

With the description of the building of the temple complete, 6.37-38
calculates the number of years between the foundations and the
completion of the work. The final WAYYIQTOL is closural.[9] It
seems evident that here the emphasis of the sentence is on the
calculation of the number of years, in contrast with 6.1. This very
difference is apparent in

Gen. 7.10

                          ויהי לשבעת הימים

                        ומי המבול היו על־הארץ

      And after seven days the floodwaters were over the land;

as compared with 7.11

                            בשנת . . .

                    ביום הזה נקבעו כל־מעינת תהום רבה

      In the year. . . on that day the springs of the great abyss were
      opened.

b. *Interruption of the WAYYIQTOL chain (with constructions
denoting background)*

§39. The narrative proper begins with a narrative WAYYIQTOL
(§8) and develops through a series of the same verbal form. This is a
well-known fact and has in any case been noted several times in the
preceding pages. Instead, we need to analyse those cases where the
chain of narrative WAYYIQTOLs (foreground constructions) is
interrupted by a construction of a different kind (background
construction, cf. 'Tense Shifts', Chapter 7). The reasons why this
happens can be listed.

§40. (1) To express an antecedent circumstance

Gen. 31

33   (Laban searches the tents of Jacob and his wives for his gods
without result: series of WAYYIQTOLs and ולא QATAL
[its negative equivalent])

34a   ורחל לקחה את־התרפים

                              ותשמם בכר הגמל

                                 ותשב עליהם

        Now Rachel had taken the teraphim
and had placed them in the camel saddle
and had sat on them.

The WAYYIQTOL-chain is broken by the opening WAW-x-QATAL
construction (§20), continued by two WAYYIQTOLs (which
comprise a 'short independent narrative', §27) expressing a prior
event. The narrative then resumes with WAYYIQTOL (v. 34b).

Some of the examples given by Joüon[40] are of the same type: 2 Sam.
18.18; 1 Kgs 22.31; 2 Kgs 4.31. He is correct in stating: 'The only way
our pluperfect can be expressed in Hebrew is to avoid the wayyiqtol
in this way' and in doubting that, generally speaking, the WAYYIQTOL
can have the value of the pluperfect.[41] It should be made clear,
though, that only when it continues the retrospective construction
WAW-x-QATAL (anterior event) does WAYYIQTOL really correspond
to the pluperfect (§141).

§41. (2) To express simultaneity

Two examples are particularly clear:

Exod. 9.23

                     ויט משה את־מטהו על־השמים

                         <u>ויהוה נתן</u> קלת וברד

    Then Moses pointed his stick towards the sky and at the same time
Yahweh sent thunder and lightning.

Exod. 10.13a

                   ויט משה את־מטהו על־ארץ מצרים

                      <u>ויהוה נהג</u> רוח קדים בארץ

    Then Moses pointed his stick towards the land of Egypt
and at the same time Yahweh sent the east wind on the land.

In both cases the transition from WAYYIQTOL to WAW-x-QATAL
emphasizes the concurrence between the actions of Moses and God.

On the other hand, if the second action had been expressed with a WAYYIQTOL it would have been presented as coming after the first.

Another good example is:

Exod. 9.33b

ויחדלו הקלות
והברד ומטר לא־נתך ארצה

Then the thunder stopped
and at the same time hail and rain no longer fell on the land.

§42. (3) To express contrast (cf. §9)

Gen. 1.5 (cf. 1.10)

ויקרא אלהים לאור יום
ולחשך קרא לילה

And God called the light 'day'
while the darkness he called 'night'.

1 Kgs 19

3b	<div dir="rtl">וינח את־נערו שם</div>
4	<div dir="rtl">והוא־הלך במדבר</div>
3b	And he (Elijah) left his servant there.
4	He instead went into the desert.

2 Kgs 5

24b	<div dir="rtl">וישלח את־האנשים וילכו</div>
25	<div dir="rtl">והוא־בא ויעמד אל־אדניו</div>

And he (Giezi) sent the men back and they left. He instead stood before his master (Elisha).

The same shift of tense, WAYYIQTOL → (WAW-)x-QATAL (note that the WAW can be omitted!), bonds together the three introductions to divine speech in the following example:

Gen. 3.14

ויאמר יהוה אלהים אל־הנחש

Then Y. God said to the serpent...

Gen. 3.16

אל־האשה אמר

Instead, to the woman he said...

Gen. 3.17

ולאדם אמר

Finally, to Adam he said. . .

(4) To express a simultaneous circumstance

§43. This function is characteristic of the simple nominal clause, usually preceded by WAW (cf. §33).

1 Sam. 17.41

וילך הפלשתי הלך וקרב אל־דוד
<u>והאיש נשא הצנה לפניו</u>

And the Philistine came on, continually getting closer to David while the shield-bearer was in front of him.

2 Kgs 8.7

ויבא אלישע דמשק
ובן־הדד מלך־ארם חלה

And Elisha reached Damascus
when Ben-Hadad king of Aram was ill.

In special cases the simple nominal clause can be introduced by והנה (§71).

§44. I have no certain examples of WAW-x-QATAL used to express the circumstance of a preceding WAYYIQTOL (but cf. §41). The case of §40 is different since there the WAW-x-QATAL construction is initial, in other words syntactically independent of the preceding WAYYIQTOL, not connected as a circumstantial clause. The only example I have presents problems of vocalization:

Judg. 4.21

ותתקע את־היתד ברקתו
ותצנח בארץ
<u>והוא־נרדם</u>
ויעף
וימת

(Jael) drove the peg in his (Sisera's) temple
and it went into the ground
—while he was asleep
and tired;
and so he died.

The vocalization shows that נִרְדָּם is understood as a participle, but some manuscripts have the QATAL נִרְדַּם (accordingly: 'When he had fallen asleep'); וַיְעַף would then be WAYYIQTOL[42] but some scholars suggest reading it as an adjective, וְיָעֵף*.[43]

§45. The narrative chain of WAYYIQTOLs is sometimes broken by a WAW-x-QATAL type construction expressing a circumstance not of the foregoing but of the following WAYYIQTOL and it can be translated by a circumstantial clause. In this case the 'x' element is probably 'casus pendens' (cf. §109.3).

2 Sam. 10.14

ובני עמון ראו כי־נס ארם

וינסו מפני אבישי

When the Ammonites saw ('now the sons of Ammon saw') that the
    Syrians had fled,
they fled from Abishai (as well).

1 Kgs 11.21

והדד שמע במצרים כי־שכב דוד עם־אבתיו ...

ויאמר הדד אל־פרעה

When Hadad heard in Egypt that David had 'fallen asleep with his
    fathers'. . . then he said to Pharaoh.

Exod. 11.10

ומשה ואהרן עשו את־כל־המפתים האלה לפני פרעה

ויחזק יהוה את־לב פרעה

ולא־שלח את־בני־ישראל מארצו

Even though Moses and Aaron had done all these marvels in front
    of Pharaoh
Yahweh still hardened Pharaoh's heart
and he (Pharaoh) did not let the Israelites leave his land.

This sentence is a concluding comment by the narrator (at the end of the section 6.2–11.10). It is reminiscent of the final comment (at the close of Jesus' public ministry) in John 12.37 τοσαῦτα δὲ αὐτοῦ σεμεῖα πεποιηκότος ἔμπροσθεν αὐτῶν οὐκ ἐπίστευον εἰς αὐτόν where the genitive absolute of the Greek corresponds to the temporal construction WAW-x-QATAL with the value of a 'protasis' in the Hebrew example.[44]

§46. (5) To express a repeated action

Exod. 18

25   ויבחר משה אנשי־חיל מכל־ישראל
                    ויתן אתם ראשים על־העם . . .
26   ושפטו את־העם בכל־עת
          את־הדבר הקשה יביאון אל־משה
            וכל־הדבר הקטן ישפוטו הם

25   And Moses chose able men from all Israel and made them
        leaders of the people. . .
26   Now they judged the people on every occasion:
        difficult problems they brought to Moses
        but any small matter they solved themselves.

The transitional WAYYIQTOL—weQATAL (inverted) marks the shift from narrative to commentary (i.e. from foreground to background), explaining the criterion used by the judges. However, the other transition weQATAL-object—(WAW-) object-YIQTOL (twice) is minor since it remains at the level of comment (cf. the transition typical of discourse, §11); the effect of the chiastic arrangement of the components is to specify the object itself, emphasizing the difference between 'difficult problems' and 'any small matter'.

Consequently, the two constructions weQATAL and WAW-x-YIQTOL mark an abrupt interruption of the narrative intended to express a comment on the event narrated. The difference between these two constructions is that WAW-x-YIQTOL adds emphasis to the element 'x', as also happens in speech (§§57-59). Other examples of the transition WAYYIQTOL → weQATAL/WAW-x-YIQTOL are:

Exod. 34.29-33 (Narrative using WAYYIQTOLs: Having come down from Sinai Moses' face was radiant. The Israelites did not go near him unless he had called them. Having spoken to them Moses covered his face with a veil. At this point the author interrupts the narrative and switches to commentary using a construction with YIQTOL (as in §34, but with *wayehi* omitted) followed by weQATAL to explain that such behaviour then became habitual).

vv. 34-35

34
וּבְבֹא מֹשֶׁה לִפְנֵי יְהוָה לְדַבֵּר אִתּוֹ
יָסִיר אֶת־הַמַּסְוֶה עַד־צֵאתוֹ
וְיָצָא וְדִבֶּר אֶל־בְּנֵי יִשְׂרָאֵל אֵת אֲשֶׁר יְצֻוֶּה

35
וְרָאוּ בְנֵי־יִשְׂרָאֵל אֶת־פְּנֵי מֹשֶׁה כִּי קָרַן עוֹר פְּנֵי מֹשֶׁה
וְהֵשִׁיב מֹשֶׁה אֶת־הַמַּסְוֶה עַל־פָּנָיו עַד־בֹּאוֹ לְדַבֵּר אִתּוֹ

34   Now when Moses went into Yahweh's presence to speak to him
he removed the veil until he left;
then he came out to tell the Israelites what had been commanded.

35   The Israelites noticed that the skin of Moses' face was radiant;[45]
then Moses put the veil back over his face until he went to speak with him.

Other similar examples are Exod. 40.40-41; 1 Sam. 7.15-17.

2 Chron. 25.14 (Amaziah brought the gods of the Edomites with him).

וַיַּעֲמִידֵם לוֹ לֵאלֹהִים
וְלִפְנֵיהֶם יִשְׁתַּחֲוֶה
וְלָהֶם יְקַטֵּר

And he set them up as gods for himself:
in front of them he would prostrate himself
and to them he would offer incense.

Accordingly, the transition from WAYYIQTOL → weQATAL or WAW-x-YIQTOL indicates the change from a single action ('narrative' or foreground) to a repeated action ('comment' or background).

§47.   These criteria explain the complex syntax of Gen. 47.20-22:

20
וַיִּקֶן יוֹסֵף אֶת־כָּל־אַדְמַת מִצְרַיִם לְפַרְעֹה
כִּי־מָכְרוּ מִצְרַיִם אִישׁ שָׂדֵהוּ
כִּי־חָזַק עֲלֵהֶם הָרָעָב
וַתְּהִי הָאָרֶץ לְפַרְעֹה

21
וְאֶת־הָעָם הֶעֱבִיר אֹתוֹ לֶעָרִים מִקְצֵה גְבוּל־מִצְרַיִם וְעַד־קָצֵהוּ

22
רַק אַדְמַת הַכֹּהֲנִים לֹא קָנָה
כִּי חֹק לַכֹּהֲנִים מֵאֵת פַּרְעֹה
וְאָכְלוּ אֶת־חֻקָּם אֲשֶׁר נָתַן לָהֶם פַּרְעֹה
עַל־כֵּן לֹא מָכְרוּ אֶת־אַדְמָתָם

20 Joseph bought all the land of Egypt for the Pharaoh
 since the Egyptians ('Egypt') had each sold his own field
 as the famine was severe for them.
 In this way the land became Pharaoh's.
21 As for the people, he assembled them ('made them pass') in
 the cities from one end of the territory of Egypt to
 the other.
22 However, he did not buy the land belonging to the priests
 because the priests had an allowance from Pharaoh
 and they ate from their allowance which Pharaoh had
 given them:
 accordingly they did not sell their lands.

The transition from the WAYYIQTOL of v. 20b ותהי הארץ to the
WAW-x-QATAL of v. 21 (ואת העם העביר) specifies what happened to
each of the 'subjects', the land and the people, mentioned as a pair in
vv. 18-19; its function, therefore, is to mark a contrast (§42). The
first (negated) QATAL of v. 22 (... לא קנה ...) has the same function in
respect of the WAYYIQTOL of v. 20 (ויקן). The two QATALs,
governed by the כי of v. 20, are 'retrospective' (§8) whereas the כי of
v. 22 introduces a comment by the writer which explains the legal
situation in respect of the priests' lands. This last כי governs a noun
clause and then weQATAL which, like the others in the preceding
paragraph, expresses a repeated action.[46]

§48. (6) To express emphasis

The historical accounts of the kings' reigns follow a common pattern.
After the date-formula (cf. §37) and the personal particulars
(expressed in noun clauses) WAYYIQTOL is used to recount the
king's deeds apart from actions the writer wishes to emphasize. 2 Kgs
18.1-10 provides some examples of this type.

Verses 4-8 are all commentary. They comprise a series of complex
noun clauses:

v. 4 הוא הסיר 'It was he who abolished. . . ' (x-QATAL,
 §6.2).

This construction is continued by a series of problematic weQATALs
denoting the past (§158 bis).

v. 5 ביהוה אלהי־ישראל בטח, 'Only in Y., God of Israel, did he
 trust'.
v. 8 הוא־הכה את־פלשתים, 'He it was who defeated the Philistines'.

In v. 7 we probably have a weQATAL of protasis modelled on the two-member syntactic pattern (cf. Exod. 33.8-10, §98):

והיה יהוה עמו

בכל אשר־יצא ישכיל

Since Y, was with him
in all that he undertook ('went out') he succeeded.

The rare WAYYIQTOLs (vv. 6, 7) are 'continuative', (§146), preceded as they are by constructions which really belong to narrative and so do not alter the basic nature of the passage, evidently a commented narrative. The narrative itself resumes in v. 9 with *wayehi* which continues the *wayehi* of v. 1.

In v. 10 the information that Samaria was taken is first given and then commented on, with repetition of the same verb, once as WAYYIQTOL then as x-QATAL, in order to place the emphasis on the date which precedes the actual QATAL:

*וַיִּלְכְּדָהּ (MT וַיִּלְכְּדֻהָ?) מקצה שלש שנים בשנת־שש לחזקיה

היא שנת־תשע להושע מלך ישראל נלכדה שמרון

And he (Shalmaneser) took it (Samaria) after three years; in the sixth year of Hezekiah which was the ninth year of Hosea, king of Israel, Samaria was taken.

The contrast between WAYYIQTOL and x-QATAL (§9) is particularly clear in this example where the two verb forms have the same root and refer to the same event.

Here are some more examples where the transition from WAYYIQTOL → x-QATAL takes place with the same intention of placing the emphasis on the element 'x':

Gen. 7

7   ויבא נח ובניו . . . אל־התבה . . .

8   מן־הבהמה הטהורה . . .

9   שנים שנים באו אל־נח אל־התבה זכר ונקבה

7   Noah and his sons. . . (all) entered the ark. . .
8   (However) pure animals. . . 9 (only) in pairs ('two by two') went into the ark with Noah, male and female.

The emphasis here is on the animals entering (only) in pairs whereas the whole of Noah's family was allowed in.

Gen. 41.12b (this is a 'narrative discourse', cf. §74)

ויפתר־לנו את־חלמתינו

איש כחלמו פתר

And he (Joseph) interpreted the dreams for us:
(for) each according to his own dream did he interpret.

Exod. 7.6 (cf. 12.28, 50)

ויעש משה ואהרן
כאשר צוה יהוה אתם כן עשו

Moses and Aaron did (this);
they did as Yahweh had commanded them.

Job 32

2   ... ויחר אף אליהוא בן־ברכאל
באיוב חרה אפו על־צדקו נפשו מאלהים
3   ובשלשת רעיו חרה אפו על־אשר לא־מצאו
מענה וירשיעו את־איוב

2 Then the anger of Elihu, son of Barachel. . . flared up: against Job
his anger flared up because he proclaimed himself upright in front
of God; 3 his anger also flared up against his three friends because
they had not found any answer but had declared Job guilty.

§49. In conclusion, the various constructions which can interrupt the
chain of narrative WAYYIQTOLs can be summarized as follows:

(1) WAYYIQTOL → WAW-x-QATAL	= anteriority (§40)	
	= simultaneity (§41)	
	= contrast (§42)	
	= emphasis (§48)	
	= circumstance of the following WAYYIQTOL (§45)	
(2) WAYYIQTOL → simple nominal clause	= contemporaneity (§43)	
(3) WAYYIQTOL → weQATAL or (WAW)-x-YIQTOL	= repetition (§46)	

From the aspect of text linguistics every construction which breaks
the narrative chain belongs to the background (emphasis, §3.2). For
an evaluation of these in terms of syntax see §126.6.

§50. I do not think there are morphological or syntactical criteria for
determining which of the five functions indicated in the previous
paragraph the WAW-x-QATAL construction can at times take on.
The only criterion is semantic: context and meaning. The weQATAL
and WAW-simple noun clause constructions, on the other hand,
appear to be custom-made for their respective functions (the first for
a repeated action, the other for a contemporaneous circumstance).

All the cases we have considered show differing degrees of transition from 'narrative' to 'comment' (or from foreground to background, §34) and show how attentive the sacred writer was to place the narrative material on different levels and as foreground or background. By these syntactic means the narrative avoids becoming a uniform and colourless series of WAYYIQTOLs, the only purely narrative form available in Hebrew.

Chapter 6

DISCOURSE

§51. Since the variety of verb forms available in discourse is greater than in narrative (§8) the different levels of communication are correspondingly more explicit. The foreground can be denoted by the jussive YIQTOL and the other volitional forms (imperative, cohortative) and by the indicative x-YIQTOL (§55), (x-)QATAL (§§22-23) and simple noun clauses; the background can be indicated by simple noun clauses, usually preceded by WAW (contemporaneity), WAW-x-QATAL (anteriority); recovered information is indicated by QATAL (preceded by כי, אשר etc.), anticipated information by indicative YIQTOL, various kinds of final clauses, etc. (cf. §3).

§52. Joshua 1

16	ויענו את־יהושע לאמר
	כל אשר־צויתנו
	נעשה
	ואל־כל־אשר תשלחנו
	נלך
17	ככל אשר שמענו אל־משה
	כן נשמע אליך
	רק יהיה יהוה אלהיך עמך
	כאשר היה עם־משה
18	כל־איש אשר־ימרה את־פיך
	ולא־ישמע את־דבריך
	לכל אשר־תצונו
	יומת
	רק חזק ואמץ

16 And they (the Israelites) answered Joshua:
   'All that you have commanded us
   we shall do
   and wherever you shall send us
   we will go;

17 just as we listened to Moses in everything
    so shall we listen to you.
    Only may Yahweh your god be with you as he was with
    Moses.
18 Whoever rebels against your orders
    and does not listen to your words
    in everything you command
    shall be put to death. Only, be strong and brave!'

This text is a good illustration of how the message looks both forward
(promise of obedience to Joshua)—indicated by YIQTOL—and back
(comparison with Moses)—indicated by QATAL.

The future perspective is indicated by the indicative YIQTOL
even if it occurs in a dependent clause, preceded by מה or אשר:

Gen. 37.20

...(§63)

ונראה מה־יהיו חלמתיו
... and we shall see what will become of his dreams!

Ruth 3

	אל־תודעי לאיש עד כלתו לאכל ולשתות
3b	
4	ויהי בשכבו
	וידעת את־המקום <u>אשר ישכב־שם</u>
	ובאת
	וגלית מרגלתיו
	ושכבתי (ketib)
	והוא יגיד לך את <u>אשר תעשין</u>

3b Do not let yourself be recognised by that man until you have
    finished eating and drinking,
4   so that when he lies down
    you will know the place where he will lie down.
    Then you shall go,
    you shall uncover the place for his feet
    and you shall lie down,
    and he will tell you what you have to do.

Note that the YIQTOL takes on the same function in narrative
(§88).

§53. Genesis 42

10   ויאמרו אליו
                  לא אדני
           ועבדיך באו לשבר־אכל
11   כלנו בני איש־אחד נחנו
               כנים אנחנו
         לא־היו עבדיך מרגלים

10 And they (Joseph's brothers) said to him:
    'No, my lord,
    instead your servants have come to buy food.
11 All of us, we are all sons of a single man;
    we are honest;
    never have your servants been spies'.

Here, instead, the operative levels of the message concern the past
(with QATAL) and the present (with simple noun clauses).

§54. Only two examples are needed to illustrate the constructions
denoting background which occur in discourse: WAW-simple noun
clause and WAW-x-QATAL:

Gen. 20.3b

                        ויאמר לו
          הנך מת על־האשה אשר־לקחת
                 <u>והא בעלת בעל</u>
And he (God) said to him (Abimelek):
'See, you shall die on account of the woman you took
because she is married'.

Gen. 24.56

                     ויאמר אלהם
                 אל־תאחרו אתי
             <u>ויהוה הצליח דרכי</u>
And he said (Abraham's servant to Rebecca's relatives):
'Do not delay me
since Yahweh has made my journey successful'.

a. *YIQTOL*

§55. It is only in verbs with final ה/י and with medial ו that the
YIQTOL, in the Qal, has two forms which are morphologically

distinct: a long form (יְהְיֶה, יָקוּם) for the indicative and a short form (יְהִי, יָקֹם) for the jussive. As for other types of verb, this distinction is sometimes found in the Hiph'il; for example, יַפְקִיד is indicative, יַפְקֵד jussive. For the most part, though, such a distinction is not clear from morphology. Even then, it is not always rigorously followed even where the distinction is possible.

Another criterion for telling apart the two forms of the YIQTOL is the corresponding negative construction, which is לא + long form of YIQTOL (sometimes termed the 'prohibitive') for the indicative, and אל + short form of YIQTOL (sometimes termed the 'vetitive') for the jussive.[47] Even this distinction, though, is not rigorously maintained in the texts. A couple of examples will be enough to prove these two statements.

Ruth 1.8b

יעשה (ketib) יהוה עמכם חסד
May Y. show mercy on you!

According to the ketib, the jussive YIQTOL is in the long form; the qere, instead, suggests reading the expected short form: יַעַשׂ.

Exodus 12

(. . . series of instructions concerning the passover lamb)

8	ואכלו את־הבשר בלילה הזה
	צלי־אש ומצות על־מררים יאכלהו
9	אל־תאכלו ממנו נא ובשל מבשל במים
	כי אם־צלי־אש
	ראשו על־כרעיו ועל־קרבו
10	ולא־תותירו ממנו עד־בקר
	והנתר ממנו עד־בקר באש תשרפו

8   They shall eat the flesh on that night;
     roasted over the fire and with unleavened bread together
          with bitter herbs shall they eat it.
9   You shall not eat any of it raw or boiled with water,
          but only roasted over the fire,
          its head, leg and entrails.
10   You shall not let anything be left over until the morning;
     anything of it that remains until morning you shall burn
     with fire.

Note that in this passage both negative constructions occur, with אל
and with לא, corresponding in context with the forms weQATAL and
indicative YIQTOL (always in second position within the sentence,
as x-YIQTOL, see below).

Since morphological criteria are evidently inadequate for distinguishing jussive YIQTOL from indicative YIQTOL, other criteria
must be found which are syntactic and linguistic. In my view two
seem particularly important: (1) the position of YIQTOL in the
sentence, (2) the connection with a preceding volitive form.[48]

1. Of importance is the fact that indicative YIQTOL never comes
first in the sentence. See, for example, Josh. 1.16-17 (§52), Deut.
10.20 (§56) and the examples cited in this paragraph. Even in the
passover instructions (cf. Exod. 12.8-10 cited above) and the
Decalogue (Exod. 20.3ff. = Deut. 5.6ff.) where indicative YIQTOL
and its corresponding negative with לא express obligations (and so
come close to the function of the jussive) in the only instance where
the verb is used positively it occurs in second position (x-YIQTOL):

Exod. 20.9 = Deut. 5.13

ששת ימים תעבד
ועשית כל־מלאכתך
For six days shall you labour
and do all your work.

To this another important fact must be added: the weYIQTOL form
is avoided when the action is to be marked only as future (i.e., not
volitive); weQATAL is used instead. In other words, the continuation
form of an initial x-YIQTOL construction (= simple future) is
weQATAL (as seen in the example just given), or WAW-x-YIQTOL,
not weYIQTOL which is the indirect jussive form (§61, cf. §§35 and
126.1). This can be seen clearly in passages which evidently contain
predictions (simple future), for example:

Exodus 7

17b   הנה אנכי מכה במטה אשר־בידי על־המים אשר ביאר
ונהפכו לדם
18   והדגה אשר־ביאר תמות
ובאש היאר
ונלאו מצרים לשתות מים מן־היאר

17b See I am going to hit, with the stick which is in my hand,
the waters which are in the Nile,
and they will change to blood
18 while the fish which are in the Nile will die.
The Nile will putrefy
and the Egyptians will not be able (any longer) to drink
the water of the Nile.

Exodus 7

27   ואם־מאן אתה לשלח
             הנה אנכי נגף את־כל־גבולך בצפרדעים
28   ושרץ היאר צפרדעים
                                      ועלו
29   ובאו בביתך... .ובבית עבדיך ובעמך ...
        ובכה ובעמך ובכל־עבדיך יעלו הצפרדעים

27   And if you refuse to let (the people) go,
     see I am about to strike all your territory with frogs.
28   The Nile will crawl with frogs
     who ('and [they]') will climb up
     and they will enter your house..., the house of your
     ministers and of your people...;
29   and against you, against your people and against all your
     ministers will the frogs climb up.

To me this is confirmation, then, that an indicative YIQTOL can
never come first in a clause. Here then is how it is distinct from a
jussive YIQTOL which, instead, normally comes first. There is no
need to provide examples for the use of the jussive form. Those cited
by Talstra in the article mentioned in note 48 will be enough: Exod.
5.9; Ruth 3.13; Deut. 20.5-8; Exod. 5.21; 1 Sam. 24.13; 2 Sam. 3.39;
Ruth 1.8, 9; 2.12; etc.

2. Some discussion is needed, though, of cases where the x-
YIQTOL construction seems to have a jussive function even though
the verbal form does not come first in the sentence. This is certainly
a possibility and the only valid criterion for making the distinction is
contextual in character. An x-YIQTOL (or WAW-x-YIQTOL)
construction can be labelled as jussive when preceded by one of the
direct volitive forms which occur in Hebrew (cohortative, imperative
and jussive).[49] Here are some examples:

Genesis 43

11 (series of imperatives)

12 וכסף משנה קחו בידכם

ואת־הכסף המושב בפי אמתחתיכם תשיבו בידכם...

13 (series of imperatives)

14 ואל שדי יתן לכם רחמים לפני האיש...

12 'Take double money with you
and take back with you the money which was replaced in the
opening of your sacks...

14 And may Shaddai grant you mercy in the presence of that
man...'

In this example the following tense shifts occur (←→ = homogeneous
shift, → = heterogeneous shift, cf. §4): (v. 11 imperatives ←→)
WAW-x-imperative → WAW-x-jussive YIQTOL (v. 12), (v. 13
imperatives →) WAW-x-jussive YIQTOL (v. 14).

Exod. 10.24

לכו

עברו את־יהוה

רק צאנכם ובקרכם יצג

גם־טפכם ילך עמכם

Go,
worship Y.!
But your flock and your cattle must be left here!
Even your children should go with you!

The tense shifts here are: imperative ←→ imperative → x-jussive
YIQTOL ←→ x-jussive YIQTOL.

Exodus 19

21 רד

העד בעם

פן־יהרסו אל־יהוה לראות

ונפל ממנו רב

22 וגם הכהנים הנגשים אל־יהוה יתקדשו

פן־יפרץ בהם יהוה

21 Go down,
warn the people
in case they break through to Y. in order to see
and so (then) many of them fall.

22   For their part, the priests who can approach Y. should
                    consecrate themselves
             in case Y. breaks through to them.

Here the tense shifts are: imperative ⟷ imperative (→ two
coordinated dependent clauses) → WAW-x-jussive YIQTOL (→
dependent clause parallel to the first of the previous two).

Other examples of the sequence direct volitive form → (WAW)-x-
jussive YIQTOL are the following: Exod. 25.2-3 (imperative → we—
indirect jussive YIQTOL ⟷ we—indirect jussive YIQTOL → x-
jussive YIQTOL, §63).

The examples seen so far show the tense shift imperative →
(WAW-)x-YIQTOL, or imperative → weYIQTOL.[50] Now, as has
been said, the (WAW-)x-YIQTOL construction here functions as a
jussive because it continues a volitive form. Elsewhere, though, when
it continues a weQATAL and alternates with it, it indicates an action
to be simple future, not volitive (cf. Exod. 7.17b-18; 7.27-29 cited
above and the examples in §§57ff.). weYIQTOL, though, is always a
volitive form in the classical language (cf. above).

From this we can deduce that even in the absence of other criteria
the very presence of weYIQTOL in second position shows the
preceding construction to be volitive as well. For example:

Exod. 27.20

ואתה תצוה את־בני ישראל
ויקחו אליך שמן זית זך כתית למאור
להעלת נר תמיד

> For your part, command the Israelites
> to (lit. so that they) bring you olive oil—pure and refined—for the
> candelabrum,
> to feed a perpetual flame.

In this instance, because the WAW-x-YIQTOL construction (ואתה
תצוה) is initial and so not preceded by a volitive form, the criterion set
out above (no. 2) cannot be applied. In view of the fact that it is
continued by a weYIQTOL (ויקחו), though, we are forced to conclude
that its function is jussive. In any case, this analysis is confirmed by
the parallel Lev. 24.2 where the text is identical, though there the
imperative צו, 'command!' replaces ואתה תצוה.

What has been said concerning YIQTOL and weYIQTOL (3rd
pers.) is also true of the cohortative (1st pers. sing. or plur.). There

are examples of the cohortative at the head of a clause: Gen. 32.21;
Deut. 12.20; 17.14; Judg. 14.12; or in second position: Exod. 32.30b.
ועתה אעלה . . . אולי אכפרה, 'But now I wish to go up. . . , perhaps I will
manage to expiate'; Num. 20.19 ברגלי אעברה, 'I wish to cross on foot';
Deut. 2.28 רק אעברה ברגלי, 'Only, I wish to cross on foot'. Sometimes
the cohortative is continued by additional cohortatives preceded by
WAW: Gen. 45.28; Exod. 4.18; 2 Kgs 6.2, cf. §61; 2 Chron. 20.9. In
addition, the x-YIQTOL construction of 1st pers. sing. or plur. (as
noted already in respect of the 3rd pers.) should be labelled a
cohortative when continued by a weYIQTOL in the same person.
For example:

Exod. 24.7b

כל אשר־דבר יהוה נעשה ונשמע

All that Y. has said we wish (or: we promise) to do and to listen
to.

If a volitive meaning had not been intended here the form would
have been weQATAL not weYIQTOL.

§56. As mentioned above (§55.1) the YIQTOL with indicative
function never comes first in the clause. This means it occurs in the
form of a construction which is a complex nominal clause, the x-
YIQTOL (with or without WAW), where the emphasis is normally
placed on the element 'x' preceding the verb (§6). Deut. 10.20 is a
particularly clear example since the complement is repeated four
times:

את־יהוה אלהך תירא
אתו תעבד
ובו תדבק
ובשמו תשבע

Yahweh your God must you revere,
him must you worship,
to him must you hold fast,
and in his name must you swear oaths.

See also the examples in §§57-60. On the syntactic status of
indicative YIQTOL see §135 (no. 5) below.

b. *weQATAL*

§57. weQATAL is an 'inverted' construction which is extremely important in discourse. It always comes first in the sentence but never occurs at the beginning of an independent narrative unit. The same applies when weQATAL occurs in narrative (cf. §§35, 46). For a discussion of this phenomenon see §135 (no. 8). Therefore, it is a continuation form. It can be preceded by a (WAW-)x-YIQTOL construction indicating the simple future, or even by a simple nominal clause (see the examples in §55.1). Often it continues an imperative as also does the weYIQTOL.

Good examples of such continuation patterns occur in the parallel sections of Exodus where God's instructions concerning the tent are then carried out by Moses. The fulfilment repeats the text of the command almost word for word but converts the discourse into narrative. It is important to note that unlike WAYYIQTOL, weQATAL does not come first in the chain, proof that it is always a continuation form. It is preceded by an imperative continued either by weYIQTOL or by x-YIQTOL.

Exodus 25

2	דבר אל־בני ישראל
	ויקחו־לי תרומה
	מאת כל־איש אשר ידבנו לבו תקחו את־תרומתי
3	וזאת התרומה אשר תקחו מאתם
	(list of precious objects: vv. 3b-7)
8	ועשו לי מקדש
	ושכנתי בתוכם
9	ככל אשר אני מראה אותך את תבנית המשכן ואת תבנית כל־כליו
	וכן תעשו

2	Command the Israelites
	to obtain an offering for me:
	from anyone who is moved by his heart to give shall you
	obtain my offering.
3	And this is the offering you shall obtain from them...
8	And so they shall make a sanctuary for me
	and I shall dwell in their midst.
9	According to all that I will show you concerning the design
	for the Tabernacle and the design of all its accoutrements,
	so shall you do.

Besides the sequence ויקחו דבר (indirect jussive, cf. §55) in v. 2 note the contrast between ויקחו and מאת כל־איש... תקחו, i.e. between weYIQTOL and x-YIQTOL. The function of this last construction is to emphasize the element 'x' which precedes the YIQTOL (§56). This function is especially clear here because the same clause is repeated (ויקחו־לי תרומה/. . .תקחו את־תרומתי) with a change of construction and the insertion of the qualifier מאת כל־איש before the second verb form. Accordingly, the repetition is not tautological but emphatic; its function is to specify the persons from whom the offerings should be taken. This interpretation is confirmed by the parallelism with the following sentence (v. 3) which has the same construction preceded by WAW: WAW-x-YIQTOL (וזאת. . .תקחו). There the emphasis falls on וזאת: the sentence specifies what should be accepted as an offering to Yahweh. The construction weYIQTOL, therefore, expresses the command in a general form (taking up the offerings), while the next two constructions—(WAW)-x-YIQTOL—specify two factors of the command (what to take and from whom).

After the sequence imperative → weYIQTOL/x-YIQTOL (vv. 2-3), comes the series of weQATALS introducing each single action (or detail of an action) to be carried out. Only rarely does WAW-x-YIQTOL replace weQATAL in this function (cf. Exod. 26.1, §58). The chain of weQATALs is only broken for a special reason. For example in v. 9 of the quoted passage ו (of apodosis) followed by כן תעשו occurs, which interrupts the chain of the two preceding we-QATALs (v. 8) precisely in order to specify clearly how these 'works' were to be carried out (i.e., exactly as specified in the pattern revealed). Then the chain is resumed in v. 10.

§58. The chain of weQATALS is what corresponds, in commentary, to the narrative chain of WAYYIQTOLs, while the 'emphatic' construction (WAW-)x-YIQTOL corresponds to (WAW)-x-QATAL as the following texts show.

Exod. 26	Exod. 36
ואת־המשכן תעשה עשר יריעת 1.	8. ויעשו כל־חכם־לב בעשי
	המלאכה את־המשכן עשר יריעת
שש משזר ותכלת וארגמן ותלעת שני	שש. . .(identical)
כרבים מעשה חשב תעשה אתם	כרבים מעשה חשב עשה אתם

You will make the Tabernacle with ten hangings; with finely woven linen, purple and scarlet, in (the form of) cherubim, the work of a seamster, shall you make them (the hangings).

26.1 begins with the construction WAW-x-YIQTOL (complex nominal clause) instead of the normal weQATAL, probably in order to emphasize the object (placed before the verb); in any case, 36.8 uses WAYYIQTOL. The function of the second construction, x-YIQTOL (26.1b, another complex nominal clause) is to emphasize whatever precedes the verb, specifying the material and the 'manufacture' of the hangings;[51] accordingly, in 36.8 x-QATAL is used. In spite of the lexical difficulties to be found in these texts[52] it is obvious that 26.1 comprises two sentences of which the second explains the first,[53] exactly as in the parallel passage, 36.8.

Exod. 26		Exod. 36	
2	ארך היריעה האחת שמנה	9 (ditto)	
	ועשרים באמה		
	ורחב ארבע באמה היריעה האחת	(ditto)	
	מדה אחת לכל־היריעת		

The length of each hanging shall be 28 cubits and in width, a hanging shall be 4 cubits; there shall be a single size for all the hangings.

Exodus 26 does not introduce a new topic but describes the hangings, already mentioned previously, using noun clauses; Exodus 36 brings the narrative to a halt, changing to comment but retaining the same noun clauses.

3	חמש היריעת תהיין	10	ויחבר את־חמש
	חברת אשה אל־אחתה		יריעת אחת אל־אחת
	וחמש יריעת		וחמש יריעת חבר
	חברת אשה אל־אחתה		אחת אל־אחת
4	ועשית ללאת תכלת על	11	ויעש ... (ditto).
	שפת היריעה האחת מקצה		
	בחברת		במחברת ...
	וכן תעשה בשפת היריעה		כן עשה ...(ditto).
	הקיצונה במחברת השנית		
5	חמשים ללאת תעשה	12	חמשים ללאת עשה ...(ditto).
	ביריעה האחת		
	וחמשים ללאת תעשה בקצה		עשה....
	היריעה אשר במחברת השנית		
	מקבילת הללאת אשה אל־אחתה		...אחת אל־אחת...
6	ועשית חמשים קרסי זהב	13	ויעש ...
	וחברת את־היריעת אשה		ויחבר ...אחת אל־אחת...
	אל־אחתה בקרסים		
	והיה המשכן אחד		ויהי ...

3   Five curtains shall be joined to each other
          and (another) five joined to each other.
4   And you shall make loops of blue (material) along the edge of
          the last curtain, along the line of the join.
          And do the same on the edge of the last curtain, along the
          second line of the join.
5   Fifty loops shall you make on one curtain,
          and fifty loops shall you make on the edge of the curtain
          which is along the second line of the join;
          the loops should match each other.
6   And you shall make fifty gold clips
          and shall join the curtains to each other with the clips.
          And so the Tabernacle will be a single unit.

In Exodus 36 WAYYIQTOL (fulfilment) replaces both the weQATAL
(command) of Exod. 26 and the initial construction x-YIQTOL
(v. 3a, with preposed object as in 26.1), while its parallel construction
(v. 3b) has been changed to the WAW-x-QATAL (36.10b) of contrast
(§42). The 'emphatic' (WAW-)x-YIQTOL type constructions, instead,
have been expressed by the corresponding (WAW-)-x-QATAL
construction: 26.4 וכן תעשה vs. 36.11 כן עשה; 26.5 חמשים ללאת תעשה vs.
36.12 וחמשים ללאת עשה (twice).

§59. The transformation of the weQATAL chain to narrative
WAYYIQTOLs is best seen in

Exodus 27		Exodus 38	
וְעָשִׂיתָ . . . 1		וַיַּעַשׂ . . . 1	
וְעָשִׂיתָ . . . 2		וַיַּעַשׂ . . . 2	
וְצִפִּיתָ . . .		וַיְצַף . . .	
וְעָשִׂיתָ . . . 3		וַיַּעַשׂ . . . 3	
וְעָשִׂיתָ . . . 4		וַיַּעַשׂ . . . 4	
וְעָשִׂיתָ . . .			

In these same two passages 'emphatic' constructions correspond as
follows: 27.1 רבוע יהיה, 'it shall be square' vs. 38.1 רבוע (with no verb;
here one would expect a QATAL as in v. 2); 27.2 ממנו תהיין קרנתיו
'part of it (i.e. of one piece with the altar) shall be its horns' vs. 38.2
ממנו היו קרנתיו; 27.3 לכל-כליו תעשה נחשת, 'all its utensils you will make
out of copper' vs. 38.3 כל-כליו עשה נחשת.

In conclusion, weQATAL is the basic tense for giving an order or
instruction; but it is not normally initial (cf. §§61ff.). A chain of

coordinated weQATALs expressing a series of orders/instructions is attested. The chain can be interrupted by a simple noun clause to describe a detail within the discourse or it can be interrupted by a compound noun clause of the (WAW-)x-YIQTOL type to emphasize a detail of this kind. The chain of narrative WAYYIQTOLs corresponds to the weQATAL chain, the (WAW-)x-QATAL construction corresponds to (WAW-)x-YIQTOL, while the simple noun clause remains unchanged.

§60. Note that the transformation of weQATAL (instruction) to WAYYIQTOL (execution) takes place when the action in question is a single action, which is usually the case. But in the following examples the situation is different as the action is either repeated or habitual.

1 Sam. 16.16 (Saul's servants said to him: Have them look for a harpist).

והיה בהיות עליך רוח־אלהים רעה
ונגן בידו
וטוב לך

So that when the evil spirit of God comes upon you,
he will strum with his hand
and you will feel well.

The execution of this advice is formulated as follows:

1 Sam. 16.23

והיה בהיות רוח־אלהים אל־שאול
ולקח דוד את־הכנור
ונגן בידו
ורוח לשאול
וטוב לו
וסרה מעליו רוח הרעה

And whenever the spirit of God came upon Saul, David would take
      up the harp
and strum with his hand
and Saul would get relief
and would feel well,
and the evil spirit would go away from him.

We find the same sequence in another example:

1 Kgs 17.4 (command)

(God said to Elijah: Go near the brook Cherith).

והיה מנחל תשתה
ואת־הערבים צויתי לכלכלך שם

And so from the torrent shall you drink;
moreover, the ravens have I commanded to provide you with
food.

1 Kgs 17.6 (fulfilment)

והערבים מביאים לו לחם ...
ומן־הנחל ישתה

The ravens used to bring food to him. . .
and from the torrent he would drink.

And again in the next example:

Exod. 18.22a

(Jethro said to Moses: Choose capable people. . .)

ושפטו את־העם בכל־עת
והיה כל־הדבר הגדל יביאו אליך
וכל־הדבר הקטן ישפטו־הם

and let them judge the people at all times
every important matter they should bring to you
but any minor matter they themselves should judge.

When the execution is narrated the same verbal forms are used but
היה is omitted as it is optional (§156):

Exod. 18.26

ושפטו את־העם בכל־עת
את־הדבר הקשה יביאון אל־משה
וכל־הדבר הקטן ישפוטו הם   (§46)

See also Num. 21.8b (command) + 21.9 (fulfilment, with the same
verbal forms).

Evidently, then, when the command concerns continuous or
habitual actions the fulfilment uses the same verbal forms as in the
command. What changes, though, is the tense of weQATAL: future
in the command (speech), repetition in the fulfilment (narrative).
This corresponds to the normal tense equivalents of weQATAL
(§§156-157).

Accordingly, we can summarize §§58-60 as follows:

Command (after the initial imperative)	Fulfilment 1 (for a single action)	Fulfilment 2 (for a repeated action)
weQATAL (WAW-)x-YIQTOL SNC	WAYYIQTOL (WAW-)x-QATAL SNC	weQATAL (WAW-)x-YIQTOL SNC
N.B. SNC = simple nominal clause		

c. *Volitive forms, weYIQTOL, weQATAL*

§61. As is well known, there are three volitive forms in Hebrew: the cohortative ('EQTeLA) for the first person, the imperative for the second, the jussive (יָקֹם) for the third. Each of these can be continued by one or more forms of the same type, by form(s) of a different type or even by an inverted weQATAL. The problem is: Can the function of each combination of verbal forms be identified? Bendavid[54] has provided a good selection of examples which we can draw on to try and sort out this delicate problem to some degree. The author classifies his examples by person and by whether the WAW is coordinate or inversive. Generally speaking it is true that when the verbal forms are in the same person the following applies.

In the first person there can be a series of cohortatives (with coordinating WAW) or continuation using weQATALTI (with inversive WAW).

In the second person there can be a series of imperatives or continuation by weQATALTA.

In the third person, continuation is by weYIQTOL or weQATAL. In the same way, when the verbal forms are in different persons, either continuative or inverted forms are possible.

Two groups of continuation constructions are therefore possible: (1) other coordinated volitive forms preceded by WAW (we'EQTeLA, UQeTOL, weYIQTOL) which we shall call indirect volitive forms in order to distinguish them from initial forms (which we shall call direct volitive forms); (2) inverted forms (weQATALTI, weQATALTA, weQATAL).

Now, both in cases where the persons are identical and where they are different it seems that the coordinated forms express the volitive aspect of the action (often with a nuance of finality), while the

inverted forms simply indicate a series of future actions. For
example, compare 2 Kgs 6.2

נלכה־נא עד־הירדן
ונקחה משם איש קורה אחת
ונעשה־לנו שם מקום לשבת שם

Let us go to the Jordan
and so that we can take a log from there
and let us make a place there for us to live in;

with Num. 13.30

עלה נעלה
וירשנו אתה

Yes, let us go up
and (= thus) occupy it (the land of Canaan).

This causative value of weQATAL finds express confirmation from a
comparison of the following two parallel passages:

1 Chron. 14.10

עלה
ונתתים בידך

2 Sam. 5.19

עלה
כי־נתן אתן את־הפלשתים בידך

Go up,
for assuredly will I place the Philistines in your hand.

We should point out a few passages which seem to be problematic,
even though the wording is similar, due to the alternation between
weQATAL and weYIQTOL after the imperative:

1 Kgs 22.6b = 2 Chron. 18.5b

עלה
ויתן אדני ביד המלך

1 Kgs 22.15b

עלה
והצלח
ונתן יהוה ביד המלך

// 2 Chron. 18.14b

עלו
והצליחו
<u>וינתנו בידכם</u>

When the rule set out above is applied, the clauses with
weYIQTOL should be translated: 'Go up, and may Adonai place (the
city) in the hand of the king!' (1 Kgs 22.6b), '. . . and may they be
placed in your hand!' (2 Chron. 18.14b); the clause with weQATAL,
though, should be translated: '. . . since Y. will place (it) in the king's
hand' (1 Kgs 22.15b).

Exod. 25.2ff., cited already (§57) is a good illustration of the
difference between weYIQTOL (aim/intention) and weQATAL
(result) which continue the initial imperative:

2a   דבר אל־בני ישראל
                           <u>ויקחו</u>־לי תרומה

(Specifications are given: what should be taken and from whom:
vv. 2b-7)

8   ועשו לי מקדש
                           ושכנתי בתוכם

2a   Command the children of Israel to take up ('Speak. . so that
          they take up') an offering for me. . .
8   And (so, with the contributions collected) they shall make
          for me a sanctuary and (so) I shall live among them.

The volitive force of weYIQTOL in Exod. 25.2a is confirmed from a
comparison with the parallel, 35.4b-5, where an imperative replaces
the weYIQTOL:

 דבר ...25.2a   35.4b זה הדבר אשר צוה יהוה לאמר
... <u>ויקחו</u>   35.5   קחו מאתכם תרומה ליהוה

35.4b   This is the word which Y. commanded, saying:
35.5   Collect from among you an offering for Y.!

The same equivalence between weYIQTOL and the imperative
occurs in the following two parallel passages:

Josh. 4.16   Josh. 4.17
... צוה את־הכהנים   ויצו יהושע את־הכהנים לאמר
<u>ויעלו</u> מן־הירדן   <u>עלו</u> מן־הירדן

Command the priests. . .	Joshua commanded the priests:
that they should climb up	'Climb up from the Jordan!'
from the Jordan. . .	

Let us also look at the next example:

Lev. 16.2

דבר אל־אהרן אחיך
ואל־יבא בכל־עת אל־הקדש . . .
ולא ימות . . .

Speak to Aaron, your brother
that he should not ('so that he should not') enter the sanctuary at
     any time
and so he will not die. . .

From this passage it is clear that the sequence דבר → ואל־יבא is the negative equivalent of the sequence imperative → weYIQTOL used in the preceding examples. The negative form with אל is further proof that weYIQTOL is a jussive (cf. §55). The construction ולא ימות (with לא!) which follows, however, is the negative equivalent of a closural weQATAL.

§62. The volitive value of weYIQTOL (indirect jussive) comes out even more clearly when it continues an initial YIQTOL (direct jussive) as in the following example:

Numbers 6

24	יברכך יהוה
	וישמרך
25	יאר יהוה פניו אליך
	ויחנך
26	ישא יהוה פניו אליך
	וישם לך שלום
27	ושמו את־שמי על־בני ישראל
	ואני אברכם

24	May Y. bless you
	and guard you,
25	may Y. make his face shine towards you
	and show you mercy,
26	may Y. 'raise his face' towards you
	and give you peace!

27   And so shall they (Aaron and his sons) place my
       name on the children of Israel,
       and I, for my part, will bless them.

Note that the chain of volitive forms (vv. 24-26) is interrupted by the
closing weQATAL construction (as well as by WAW-x-YIQTOL to
mark the equivalence between the God's action and the priests'
action). Remember that the tense shift weQATAL → WAW-x-
YIQTOL is typical of speech (§11).

The complicated text Gen. 41.33-36, where two parallel series of
coordinated jussives occur, both of which conclude with the inverted
forms weQATAL, can also be explained along these lines.

33 (1)	ועתה ירא פרעה איש נבון וחכם
	וישיתהו על־ארץ מצרים
34	יעשה פרעה
	ויפקד פקדים על־הארץ
	וחמש את־ארץ מצרים בשבע שני השבע
35 (2)	ויקבצו את־כל־אכל השנים הטבת הבאת האלה
	ויצברו־בר תחת יד־פרעה אכל בערים
	ושמרו
36	והיה האכל לפקדון לארץ בשבע שני
	הרעב אשר תהין בארץ מצרים
	ולא־תכרת הארץ ברעב

33   And therefore, let Pharaoh choose an intelligent and wise
       man
       and set him (= in order to set him) over the land of
       Egypt.
34   Let Pharaoh act
       and appoint (= see to appointing) inspectors over the land
       and (so) he will be able to tax by a fifth the land of Egypt
       during the seven years of plenty.
35   And let them (the inspectors) collect all the food of
       those
       good years which are coming
       and let them store the grain under Pharaoh's control for
       food
       in the cities
       and (so) they will be able to preserve (it).
36   And the food shall be in reserve for the country for the
       seven years of famine which will come about in the land of
       Egypt
       and the land shall not be destroyed by the famine.

The two series of jussives express the measures needed to be taken and the weQATALS express the result required to combat the famine. Accordingly, the text is perfectly intelligible as it stands (contrast BHK and BHS).

§63. The contrast between weYIQTOL expressing intention ('volitive' future) and weQATAL expressing result (simple future) is evident in Exodus 14.

דבר אל־בני ישראל 2
וישבו
ויחנו לפני פי החירת בין מגדל ובין הים לפני בעל צפן
נכחו תחנו על־הים
ואמר פרעה לבני ישראל 3
נבכים הם בארץ
סגר עליהם המדבר
וחזקתי את־לב־פרעה 4
ורדף אחריהם
ואכברה בפרעה ובכל־חילו
וידעו מצרים כי־אני יהוה (cf. vv. 17-18)

2 Tell the people of Israel
that they should turn back
and that they should camp in front of Pi-hahiroth, between Migdol and the sea,
in front of Baal Zaphon:
in front of it you shall camp near the sea.
3 And (when/since) Pharaoh shall say of the people of Israel:
'They are lost in the land
the desert has trapped them'
4 then I shall harden the heart of Pharaoh
who shall pursue them ('and he will pursue them')
so that I may be glorified over Pharaoh and all his forces;
and so Egypt shall know that I am Yahweh.

The opening imperative is continued by two 'volitive' weYIQTOLs (and then by the 'emphatic' x-YIQTOL construction: cf. §§57-60). The weYIQTOL chain is then broken by three weQATALS, the first a 'protasis' (ואמר), the other two (וחזקתי, ורדף) 'apodoses'. It is reasonable to suppose that the following weYIQTOLs and weQATALs have functions analogous to the others: they denote purpose and the simple future (conclusion) respectively.

A similar alternation of weYIQTOL-weQATAL and of their respective functions also occurs in Gen. 37.20:

ועתה לכו ונהרגהו
<u>ונשלכהו</u> באחד הברות
<u>ואמרנו</u>
חיה רעה אכלתהו
<u>ונראה</u> מה־יהיו חלמתיו

And now, come on, let us kill him
('go and let us kill him') and let us throw him into one of the pits;
then we shall say
that a wild beast has devoured him;
and we will see (or: 'so we may see') what will become of his
    dreams!

§64. The conclusion to be drawn is that a communication which begins with an imperative or other volitive form, continues with a weYIQTOL if the action is to be presented as volitive also (usually in the sense of intent); if, instead, the action is simply presented as future (as successive or conclusive) weQATAL is used. Even though the semantic difference between intent and succession versus conclusion is often rather slim, the regular use of the two different constructions makes identification of the two functions fairly probable. This is how Hebrew can indicate modal nuances which modern languages express by the addition of 'want to, be able to, must', etc. It is worth noting that this very distinction between weYIQTOL and weQATAL is in line with classical prose where weYIQTOL is exclusively volitive (§55).

At this stage we can summarize all that has been said, from §55 on, concerning YIQTOL and its fellow forms weYIQTOL and weQATAL in four statements.

1. A YIQTOL which comes first in the sentence is always jussive whereas indicative YIQTOL always comes in second position (x-YIQTOL, §55.1).

2. The weYIQTOL is always a(n indirect) volitive form. It can be a coordinated construction when it continues a direct volitive in the same person (Num. 6.24-26, §62), or it can be a dependent construction of purpose (and so equivalent to a final clause), especially when preceded by an imperative (imperative → weYIQTOL, cf. Exod. 25.2-3, §57; 14.2,

§63). The weYIQTOL is thus distinct from weQATAL which always indicates a simple future of succession or conclusion (cf. examples in §§62-63).

3. The (waw-)x-YIQTOL construction is jussive when preceded by a direct volitive form, for example, imperative → (WAW-) x-YIQTOL (Exod. 10.24; 19.21-22; §55.2). Likewise, it is jussive when followed by a weYIQTOL, that is, in the sequence x-YIQTOL → weYIQTOL (Exod. 27.20; 24.7b; §55.2).

4. Conversely, the (WAW-)x-YIQTOL construction is indicative when preceded by a weQATAL (Exod. 7.17b-18; 7.27-29; etc., §55.2).

For discussion of weQATAL, YIQTOL and (WAW-)x-YIQTOL in the apodosis see §135 (no. 12).

§65. The examples we have looked at so far deal with verb forms in different persons—first, second or third either mixed or, if identical, only in the first and second persons. In the case of sets of verb forms all in the second person the matter is not so clear. In some examples the difference between coordinate forms and inverted forms can be seen:

Numbers 27

12	ויאמר יהוה אל־משה
	עלה אל־הר העברים הזה
	וראה את־הארץ אשר נתתי לבני ישראל
13	וראיתה אתה
	ונאספת אל־עמיך גם־אתה
	כאשר נאסף אהרן אחיך

12 And Yahweh said to Moses:
  'Go up this mountain of Abarim
  and see the land which I have given to the people of Israel.
13 When you have seen it
  you shall be gathered ('And you shall see it and you shall be gathered) to your ancestors, you as well, as Aaron your brother was gathered'

Compare the parallel passage, Deuteronomy 32

49	עלה . . .
	וראה . . .
50	ומת בהר אשר אתה עלה שמה
	והאסף אל־עמיך . . .

> 49 Go up. . . and see. . . 50 and die on the mountain which you are
> going to climb and be gathered to your ancestors. . .

Whereas in Deuteronomy 32 there is an unbroken series of
imperatives in Numbers 27 the sequence. . . וראה. . . עלה is interrupted
by repetition of the second verb in the inverted form וראית which is
connected syntactically with the following ונאספת in the manner of
protasis-apodosis. Evidently the inverted form breaks the tight
sequence of imperatives and introduces the aspect of succession.

In other examples, however, there is no obvious difference
between coordinated and inverted forms; for example, between 1 Kgs
18.8 לך אמר לאדניך 'Go, say to your master' (cf. v. 14) and 2 Sam. 7.5
לך ואמרת אל־עבדי אל־דוד 'Go and say to my servant, David'. And two
verses earlier (2 Sam. 7.3): לך עשה 'Go, do'.

d. (ו)הנה, (ו)עתה

§66.   Besides the verb forms already studied (YIQTOL, direct and
indirect volitive forms, nominal clauses) there is a whole series of
pronouns and suffixes typical of discourse, in particular those in the
first and second person functioning 'anaphorically' (referring to
persons or events previously mentioned), 'cataphorically' (with
future reference) or 'deictically' (referring to the level of communication).[55] The so-called 'macro-syntactic markers', which denote the
subdivisions and the relationships between different parts of the text,
must also be mentioned.[56] The most important of these markers are
(ו)הנה and (ו)עתה.

(1) והנה/הנה

§67.   In prose, הנה or והנה[57] can precede the different kinds of noun
clause, even when circumstantial, and QATAL. The few examples
with YIQTOL[58] are poetic.

It should be noted that all the constructions preceded by הנה also
occur without this particle, but then the information value changes
considerably. The function of הנה is to link the past or present event
very closely with the actual moment/time of the discourse. Without
הנה the same event would be introduced as information of no
significance for the actual moment of communication.

Genesis 27

5   ורבקה שמעת בדבר יצחק אל־עשו בנו
                  וילך עשו השדה לצוד ציד להביא
6   ורבקה אמרה אל־יעקב בנה לאמר
     <u>הנה שמעתי</u> את־אביך מדבר אל־עשו אחיך לאמר
7   הביאה לי ציד
                        ועשה־לי מטעמים
                             ואכלה
              ואברככה לפני יהוה לפני מותי
8   <u>ועתה</u> בני שמע בקולי לאשר אני מצוה אתך

5 Now Rebecca was listening when Isaac spoke to his son Esau.
Esau went into the countryside to hunt game to bring back.
6 Meanwhile, Rebecca spoke as follows to her son Jacob: 'Well, I
heard your father speaking to Esau your brother as follows:

> 'Bring me back some game
> and prepare me a tasty dish
> so I may eat it
> and bless you in front of Y. before my death'

So, my son, listen to me regarding what I order you'

The information that Rebecca heard Jacob's request to Esau is
narrated as 'prior event' (with the construction WAW-x-participle:
§19) to the main action which follows (expressed by WAYYIQTOL,
continued by WAW-x-QATAL indicating simultaneity, cf. §41).
Then the same information is given in direct speech with הנה שמעתי
and so it becomes significant for the present situation as it requires a
continuation or a result. This result is introduced by ועתה.
    Without הנה, though, the information would not demand a
continuation of this kind, as the example Deut. 5.28(25b) shows:

<u>שמעתי</u> את־קול דברי העם הזה אשר דברו
אליך היטיבו כל־אשר דברו

I heard the 'voice' of the words which this people spoke to you: all
they have said is good.

§68. The meaning of a noun clause is also determined by whether or
not it is introduced by הנה.

Num. 13.29

<u>עמלק</u> יושב בארץ הנגב
והחתי והיבוסי והאמרי יושב ההר
והכנעני ישב על־הים ועל יד הירדן

(The spies report): 'The Amalekites live in the land of the Negev;
the Hittites, Jebusites and Amorites live in the mountain region:
the Canaanites live near the sea and along the Jordan.

Here the noun clauses are used for reporting the information on the
promised land collected by the spies; this information, though, is
given without reference of any kind to the actual discourse in
progress.

On the other hand, the same type of noun clause (noun-participle),
this time preceded by הנה, is used in 2 Sam. 19 to mark an event of
dramatic importance for the actual moment of discourse. The news
that David had gone into mourning and had wept over Absalom's
death is first related with the use of narrative forms.

2 Sam. 19.1a

וירגז המלך
ויעל על־עלית השער
ויבך

The king was upset
and climbed to the upper room of the gate
and wept.

It is then reported to Joab in these terms:

2 Sam. 19.2

הנה המלך בכה
ויתאבל על־אבשלם

See, the king is crying and is in mourning because of Absalom!

The construction הנה-name-participle describes an action which is
happening at the very moment of the communication; the construction continues with WAYYIQTOL, and surprising as this might
seem at first, there is no need for emendation.[59] Instead the
WAYYIQTOL should be set alongside analogous WAYYIQTOLs,
for example those which continue a QATAL in 'narrative discourse'
(cf. §76). Not only did the two actions introduced by הנה (the king's
weeping and mourning) take place at that very moment, they also
had a dangerous effect on the morale of David's soldiers (vv. 3-4).
This is why Joab went to the king and warned him of the
consequences of his actions (vv. 6-8). David listened to him and sat
in the gate. As in vv. 1-2, first the event is narrated and then reported
with the use of הנה:

2 Sam. 19.9

ויקם המלך
וישב בשער
ולכל־העם הגידו לאמר
הנה המלך יושב בשער
ויבא כל־העם לפני המלך

The king got up
and sat at the gate.
Now they informed all the people:
'See, the king is sitting at the gate!'
Then all the people came into the king's presence.

The importance of the event is also stressed by the construction ולכל־העם הגידו which interrupts the narrative in order to place the emphasis on the complement preceding the verb (cf. §48). In this way the king's new gesture cancels his previous action and reconciles him with the soldiers.

§69. Much the same happens when a noun clause is a circumstantial construction modifying the main verb in the narrative. The circumstantial clause itself is timeless and its tense is determined by the verb on which it depends. If preceded by הנה, however, it has a direct connection with that particular stage of the narrative for which it becomes important.

Gen. 18.8

ויקח חמאה וחלב ובן־הבקר אשר עשה
ויתן לפניהם
והוא־עמד עליהם תחת העץ
ויאכלו

8 Then he (Abraham) took butter, milk and the calf which he had prepared
and set them in front of them (the three visitors),
while he stood in front of them under the tree.
And they ate.

Gen. 24.30b

ויבא אל־האיש
והנה עמד על־הגמלים על־העין

And he (Laban) went to that man (Abraham's servant)
and he, in fact, was standing near the camels next to the well.

In 18.8 עמד והוא expresses a simple circumstance of the main action (§43). In 24.30b, though, והנה עמד[60] emphasizes this circumstance as exceptional since Abraham's servant had helped Rebecca at the well and had loaded her with gifts (24.28-30a). That is why Laban is quick to invite her home.

§70.   Accordingly, הנה(ו) is an important element in discourse with the function of introducing a past (§67) or present (§68) event, or a circumstance (§69) which has special relevance in respect of the actual moment of communication.

§71.   While הנה(ו) is undoubtedly used mostly in discourse it should be pointed out that it also occurs in narrative (§69). Genesis 37 provides three examples.

15
וימצאהו איש
<u>והנה</u> תעה בשרה
וישאלהו האיש לאמר
מה־תבקש

And a man found him (Joseph)
and 'behold (= while he) was wandering the countryside
Accordingly, that man asked him
'What are you looking for?'

25
וישבו לאכל־לחם
<u>וישאו</u> עיניהם
<u>ויראו</u>
<u>והנה</u> ארחת ישמעאלים באה מגלעד
וגמליהם נשאים נכאת וצרי ולט
הולכים להוריד מצרימה . . .
26   ויאמר יהודה אל־אחיו . . .

25 They (Joseph's brothers) sat down to eat,
raised their eyes
and saw: and there was a caravan of Ishmaelites coming from Gilead and camels carrying resin, balsam and laudanum, travelling to take them down to Egypt.
26 Then Judah said to his brothers. . .

29
וישב ראובן אל־הבור
<u>והנה</u> אין־יוסף בבור
ויקרע את־בגדיו

Reuben returned to the pit
but, in fact, Joseph was not in the pit.
And he tore his clothes.

Clearly והנה marks a new event and the very introduction by this particle makes it stand out arrestingly in the otherwise linear development of events. The use of הנה is connected, explicitly (v. 25) or implicitly (vv. 15, 29) with the verb 'to see'. In this way the narrative approaches the immediacy of speech. Note also that, as with speech (§67), the circumstance introduced by והנה is always very closely connected with the ensuing action: v. 15, the man's question: vv. 26-27, Judah's suggestion; v. 29, Reuben's action.

§72. Finally, let me point out that הנה(ו) occurs in the commenting formula used occasionally to conclude the historical accounts of the kings in [the books of] Chronicles; [the books of] Kings use הלא instead.[61]

1 Kgs 15.23	2 Chron. 16.11
ויתר כל־דברי אסא וכל־גבורתו	והנה דברי אשא הראשונים
. . . .	והאחרונים
הלא־המה כתובים על־ספר	הנם כתובים על־ספר
דברי הימים למלכי יהודה	המלכים ליהודה וישראל

Herewith the acts of Asa, both first and last, see they are written in the book of the kings of Judah and Israel.

2 Chron. 25.26 even has הלא הנם כתובים where the parallel, 2 Kgs 14.18, has הלא־המה כתובים.

2. עתה(ו)

§73. Unlike הנה(ו), עתה(ו) (more often with, but sometimes without ו) only occurs in speech. It is an important particle which introduces the result arising or the conclusion to be drawn concerning the present action from an event or topic dealt with beforehand. Its force, therefore, is as an adverbial expression of time with logical force: 'And now, and so'.[59]

Sometimes עתה(ו) occurs together with הנה(ו) to introduce the result of the event expressed by עתה(ו) itself. A good example is Gen. 27.6-8 (discussed above, §67); see also 1 Sam. 8.5. Other examples of עתה(ו) are examined in the next paragraph.

e. 'Narrative discourse'

§74. Occasionally a text which can be classified as speech includes a narrative section when the speaker wishes to report certain events he considers important for the actual situation. I use the term 'narrative discourse' for this type of narrative in which the events are not reported in a detached way, as in a historian's account, but from the speaker's point of view. Naturally, verbal forms in the first and second person predominate. Understood in this way, 'discourse' is the opposite of pure 'narration', or—in the terminology used by some linguists, 'Bericht'/'discours' is contrasted with 'Erzählung'/'narration' (§22). Weinrich, instead, refers to 'a narrative in the form of direct speech' or to 'oral narratives'.[63]

We now wish to examine the way in which pure speech becomes an 'account' and see whether the use of verb forms in such 'accounts' exactly matches what has been determined for narrative proper.

§75. Judg. 11.1-28, the narrative frame of which has already been looked at (§28), contains an elaborate diplomatic treaty between Jephtah and an Ammonite king (vv. 12-28) and provides us with a good example of the foregoing.

Judges 11

12	וישלח יפתח מלאכים אל־מלך בני־עמון לאמר
	מה־לי ולך כי באת אלי להלחם בארצי
13	ויאמר מלך בני־עמון אל־מלאכי יפתח
(1)	כי־לקח ישראל את־ארצי בעלותו ממצרים
	מארנון ועד־היבק ועד־הירדן
(2)	ועתה השיבה אתהן בשלום

12 Jephthah sent messengers to the king of the Ammonites saying:
'What is the matter between me and you that you have come against me to wage war in my territory?'
13 The king of the Ammonites answered Jephthah's messengers:
'Because Israel took my land when it came up from Egypt
—from the Arnon up to the Jabbok and the Jordan.
And now give them (the cities of that territory) back in peace'.

The dialogue opens with a well-known idiomatic formula (v. 12b). The reply of the king of Ammon begins with a reminder of a past event expressed by כי plus 'retrospective' QATAL (1), the basis for the conclusion introduced by the ועתה of reasoning (2). Jephtah's

new and lengthy message takes up the two points made by the
Ammonite king: first (1) using history to deny his opponent's opinion
by recounting the events which followed the Exodus, or at least those
directly affecting the argument (vv. 15-21); then (2) deriving the
conclusions from his presentation of these events (vv. 23-27). The
first point includes a long narrative which has been incorporated
within the speech.

14	ויסף עוד יפתח וישלח מלאכים אל־מלך בני־עמון
15	ויאמר לו
	כה אמר יפתח
(1)	לא־לקח ישראל את־ארץ מואב ואת־ארץ בני־עמון
16	כי־בעלותם ממצרים
	וילך ישראל במדבר עד־ים־סוף
	ויבא קדשה
17	וישלח ישראל מלאכים אל־מלך אדום לאמר
	אעברה־נא בארצך
	ולא שמע מלך אדום
	וגם אל־מלך מואב שלח
	ולא אבה
	וישב ישראל בקדש
18	וילך במדבר
	ויסב את־ארץ אדום ואת־ארץ־מואב
	ויבא ממזרח־שמש לארץ מואב
	ויחנון בעבר ארנון
	ולא־באו בגבול מואב
	כי ארנון גבול מואב
19	וישלח ישראל מלאכים אל סיחון מלך האמרי מלך חשבון
	ויאמר לו ישראל
	נעברה־נא בארצך עד־מקומי
20	ולא־האמין סיחון את־ישראל עבר בגבלו
	ויאסף סיחון את־כל־עמו
	ויחנו ביהצה
	וילחם עם־ישראל
21	ויתן יהוה אלהי־ישראל את־סיחון ואת־כל־עמו ביד ישראל
	ויכום
	ויירש ישראל את כל־ארץ האמרי יושב הארץ ההיא
22	ויירשו את כל־גבול האמרי
	מארנון ועד־היבק ומן־המדבר ועד־הירדן
23	ועתה יהוה אלהי ישראל הוריש את־האמרי מפני עמו ישראל
(2)	ואתה תירשנו
24	הלא את אשר יורישך כמוש אלהיך
	אותו תירש
	ואת כל־אשר הוריש יהוה אלהינו מפנינו

אותו נירש

25 וְעַתָּה הַטוֹב טוֹב אַתָּה מִבַּלָק בֶּן־צִפּוֹר מֶלֶךְ מוֹאָב
הֲרוֹב רָב עִם־יִשְׂרָאֵל
אִם נִלְחֹם נִלְחַם בָּם

26 בְּשֶׁבֶת יִשְׂרָאֵל בְּחֶשְׁבּוֹן וּבִבְנוֹתֶיהָ וּבְעַרְעוֹר
וּבִבְנוֹתֶיהָ וּבְכָל־הֶעָרִים אֲשֶׁר עַל־יְדֵי
אַרְנוֹן שְׁלֹשׁ מֵאוֹת שָׁנָה
וּמַדּוּעַ לֹא־הִצַּלְתֶּם בָּעֵת הַהִיא

27 וְאָנֹכִי לֹא־חָטָאתִי לָךְ
וְאַתָּה עֹשֶׂה אִתִּי רָעָה לְהִלָּחֶם בִּי
יִשְׁפֹּט יְהוָה הַשֹּׁפֵט הַיּוֹם בֵּין בְּנֵי יִשְׂרָאֵל
וּבֵין בְּנֵי עַמּוֹן

28 וְלֹא שָׁמַע מֶלֶךְ בְּנֵי עַמּוֹן אֶל־דִּבְרֵי יִפְתָּח
אֲשֶׁר שָׁלַח אֵלָיו

14 Jephthah again sent messengers to the king of the Ammonites
15 and said to him:
'So says Jephthah.'
(1) 'Israel took neither the land of Moab nor the land of the Ammonites.
16 For, when they came up out of Egypt
Israel went through the desert as far as the reed sea and came to Qadesh.
17 Then Israel sent messengers to the king of Edom saying:
'Let me pass through your land'
but the king of Edom did not listen.
To the king of Moab also (Israel) sent (messengers)
but he did not consent.
And Israel stayed in Qadesh.
18 Then went through the desert,
went round the land of Edom and the land of Moab
and arrived on the east side of the land of Moab
and camped on the other side of the Arnon
And so they did not enter Moab territory
for the Arnon is the Moab border.
19 Then Israel sent messengers to Sihon, king of the Amorites, king of Heshbon
And Israel said to him:
'Let us pass through your land to our own country'.
20 But Sihon did not believe that Israel would (only) pass through his territoty.
Sihon assembled all the people
and they camped in Jahaz
and fought with Israel.

21 However, Yahweh, God of Israel, delivered Sihon and all his people into the hand of Israel and they (Israel) defeated them. And Israel took possession of all the land of the Amorites living on that land

22 So Israel took possession of all the territory of the Amorites from the Arnon to the Yabbok and from the desert to the Jordan.

23 Therefore, it was Yahweh, God of Israel, who dispossessed the
(2) Amorites in the presence of his people Israel and will you take possession of it?

24 Isn't it true that what Chemosh your god dispossesses for you is what you will gain possession of and all that Yahweh our God has dispossessed before us we shall possess (it)?

25 So then, are you really better than Balak son of Zippor, king of Moab? Did he quarrel with Israel or fight against them?

26 While Israel resides in Heshbon and its dependencies, in Aroer and its dependencies and in all the cities which have been on both banks of the Arnon for three hundred years why didn't you regain them in that time?

27 Now for my part I have not sinned against you whereas you do me wrong by fighting against me! May Yahweh the judge adjudicate today between the Israelites and the Ammonites!'

28 But the king of the Ammonites did not listen to the words Jephthah sent him.

Jephthah's message begins and ends with phrases exclusive to speech: v. 15b... כה אמר is the well-known 'messenger formula' common in the prophetic writings: v. 23 ועתה introduces Jephthah's first conclusion (cf. v. 13) which comprises two complex noun clauses, one with QATAL (הריש) for a past action, the other with YIQTOL (תירשנו) for an action in the future, both emphasizing the two contrasted subjects: Yahweh-you (thou); v. 24: two more compound noun clauses preceded by the particle הלא and both using the two-member syntactic construction with 'casus pendens' (cf. §104) to emphasize the object which precedes the verb form (cf. §124): את אשר + YIQTOL (future) / QATAL (past) in the first member, אותו + YIQTOL in the second; v. 25: the second ועתה introduces a new conclusion expressed by two parallel verb clauses with inf. abs. + QATAL of the same verbal root; v. 26: 'two-member syntactic construction', with a temporal clause (בשבת ישארל . . .) in the protasis and ומדוע in the apodosis (cf. §102); v. 27: two noun clauses (the first a compound noun clause) with strong emphasis on the contrasted subjects ואנכי and ואתה; the last sentence of the speech uses the jussive form ישפט.

A long narrative has been inserted into this segment of pure discourse; it begins with לא־לקח ישראל (v. 15), a firm denial of the contrary thesis כי־לקח ישראל (v. 13) based on history (v. 16): כי + the 'two-member syntactic construction', with the protasis בעלותם ממצרים and the apodosis. . . וילך ישראל (cf. §102). The account continues with a chain of WAYYIQTOLs and its corresponding negation ולא + QATAL and direct speech is used twice (vv. 17, 19). The narrative chain is only interrupted in v. 17 וישלח ישראל מלאכים אל מלך אדום / וגם אל־מלך מואב שלח (WAAYIQTOL—WAW-x-QATAL) occurs, probably for contrast, as is also the case in pure narrative (§42), or at least in order to present the two treaties (with Edom and with Moab) as parallel events and not simply as successive. Further, in two instances (vv. 18 and 22) the WAYYIQTOL and its corresponding negation ולא + QATAL mark the conclusion to what has gone before, as is sometimes also the case in pure narrative (cf. §38). In v. 18, ולא־באו בגבול מואב is not, in fact, a continuation of the story but a conclusion drawn from וישב . . . את־ארץ מואב which precedes it, with the addition of the geographical rider כי ארנון גבול מואב (כי + noun clause).

Similarly, in v. 22 ויירשו repeats the ויירש of v. 21, drawing the appropriate conclusion in geographical terms. As far as content is concerned, v. 18 clearly ends the first part of the account dealing with Edom and Moab, specifying that Israel did not invade Moab territory (so that it is not true that 'Israel took the land of Moab', v. 15), while v. 22 concludes the second part which concerns Sihon, pointing out that the territory which the king of Ammon claims as his own (cf. v. 13, with an almost identical border formula) had been taken from the Amorites by Israel (and therefore 'Israel did not take. . the land of the Ammonites', v. 15).

§76. The text of Judges 11 just examined shows that QATAL is the verb form for beginning 'narrative discourse'. The same initial QATAL is found in the 'report' or 'discourse' (§§22-23); its negative form is לא + QATAL (cf. v. 15 לא־לקח). This QATAL can come first in the sentence or can be preceded by the subject (§77), like the 'report' QATAL. Once it has been introduced by QATAL the account continues with a chain of WAYYIQTOLs, as in pure narrative.

Now here a basic fact must be emphasized. No 'narrative discourse' begins with a WAYYIQTOL; the WAYYIQTOL is always the continuation form of an initial construction typical of discourse (cf. §24). This is also true in Deuteronomy 1–4 where a long series of WAYYIQTOLs (chiefly 1st pers. sing. or plur.) is used. The long 'narrative discourse' begins with this very x-QATAL construction:

Deut. 1.6a

יהוה אלהינו דבר אלינו בחרב לאמר
Y. our God spoke to us on Horeb as follows.

Direct speech follows (vv. 6b-8). The first WAYYIQTOL occurs in v. 9 (וַאֹמַר). This fact reveals the fundamental difference between the WAYYIQTOL of narrative—which is either initial or the continuation of another initial WAYYIQTOL—and the WAYYIQTOL of discourse which is never initial but always the continuation of a non-narrative initial construction, different, that is, from WAYYIQTOL (§146).

§77. As in pure narrative the chain of WAYYIQTOLs is not interrupted without a reason. We have already seen the example Judg. 11.17 (§75). We can add Deut. 5.2-5:

2	יהוה אלהינו כרת עמנו ברית בחרב
3	לא את־אבתינו כרת יהוה את־הברית הזאת
	כי אתנו אנחנו אלה פה הים כלנו חיים
4	פנים בפנים דבר יהכם עמכם בהר מתוך האש
5	אנכי עמד בין־יהוה וביניכם בעת ההיא
	להגיד לכם את־דבר יהוה
	כי יראתם מפני האש
	ולא־עליתם בהר

2 Y. our God made a covenant with us on Horeb.
3 Not with our fathers did Y. make this covenant but with us, with us here, today, all still alive.
4 Face to face Y. spoke with us on the mountain from the heart of the fire.
5 I was between Y. and you at that time, to pass on Yahweh's word to you
since you were afraid of the fire
and did not climb the mountain.

Although not introduced by כי, in the context, this short 'narrative speech' provides the motivation for the command to observe the laws transmitted by Moses (v. 1). The account begins with QATAL preceded by the subject and instead of continuing with WAYYIQTOL it continues with two x-QATALs for emphasis on the element 'x'. In v. 3 this element is part negative, אל את־אבתינו and part positive...
כי אתנו אנחנו, both parts sharply contrasted but sharing the same QATAL. Note the transition in v. 5 to a simple noun clause without WAW to express a synchronous action.

We should add that besides (x-)QATAL, as in the examples discussed so far, 'narrative discourse' can also begin with a simple nominal clause of the type noun + participle. Note that in the next example the participle is syntactically the equivalent of אשר + QATAL (§6.1):

Joshua 24

17
כי יהוה אליהנו
הוא המעלה אתנו ואת־אבותינו מארץ
מרצים מבית עבדים
ואשר עשה לעינינו את־האתות הגדלות האלה
וישמרנו בכל־הדרך אשר הלכנו בה
ובכל העמים אשר עברנו בקרבם

18
ויגרש יהוה את־כל־העמים . . .

17   Since Y. is our God
it was he who brought us and our fathers out of the land of Egypt, from the house of slaves,
and performed, before our very eyes, all those great marvels (lit. signs)
and guarded us on every road we went on and among all the peoples we passed through

18   And Y. drove out all the peoples...

Lastly, 'narrative discourse' can begin with a simple nominal clause without a participle:

Exodus 6

2b
אני יהוה

3
וארא אל־אברהם

2b   I am Y.
3   I appeared to Abraham...

§78. Finally, let us examine the narrative discourse of Gen. 44.18-34 in summary form because there as well we find *wayehi* which we know to be typical of pure narrative (§28). After requesting permission to speak (v. 18). Judah begins his account with: אדני שאל את־עבדיו לאמר (i.e. with QATAL preceded by the subject, §77); a series of WAYYIQTOLs of the verb אמר in the first and second person follows to introduce the 'narrated' dialogue: vv. 20 ונאמר, 21 ותאמר, 22 ונאמר, 23 ותאמר. The account of the dialogue in Canaan between the brothers and Jacob which follows is introduced by *wayehi*, which—syntactically considered—behaves exactly as in narrative (cf. §31).

24   ויהי כי עלינו אל־עבדך אבי
      ונגד־לו את דברי אדני

When, later, we had gone up to your servant my father we related to him the words of my master.

The dialogue continues with two further WAYYIQTOLs of the verb אמר (vv. 26, 27). Finally, Judah presents his own conclusions and suggestions, based on the preceding account, to Joseph, introducing them with two ועתה (vv. 30, 33).

We can conclude our study of 'narrative discourse' by replying to the questions posed at the start (§74).

(1) 'Narrative discourse' begins with a (foreground) construction as is normal in pure discourse: either QATAL in first position or its equivalent, x-QATAL, or even with a simple noun clause (with or without a participle).

(2) It then switches to WAYYIQTOL and continues with a chain of the same verbal form. As in narrative proper, this chain is only broken when the author wishes to shift information to a linguistic level other than the main level. The fundamental difference with respect to narrative is that WAYYIQTOL never ever begins 'narrative discourse'. Such a WAYYIQTOL, therefore, is not a narrative form but a continuation form. It is never used to open a speech unit and so has no tense of its own, taking on, instead the tense of the preceding discourse form (when it continues an (x-)QATAL or a simple noun clause with a participle) or the tense of the discourse context (when it continues a simple noun clause without a participle).

Chapter 7

TENSE SHIFT

§79. The following terminology and analysis are based, as stated earlier (§3), on Weinrich's linguistic model. According to Weinrich the value of tenses can be described from three different aspects: linguistic attitude, which reveals two levels in the text: comment/narrative; linguistic perspective, with three levels: recovered (old) information/degree zero/anticipatory information; and emphasis, at two levels: foreground/background. Every text progresses through a series of tense shifts, i.e. by means of a series of changes from one verbal form to another. The transitions are uniform when there is a succession of verb forms all belonging to the same linguistic perspective; otherwise they are not uniform. Weinrich[64] uses the term 'tense shift' for the change from one verb form to another within the same linguistic perspective. The tense shift which, instead involves two different perspectives is termed 'temporal metaphor' by Weinrich;[65] for example, the shift from pluperfect to the present tense alters both the linguistic attitude (from narrative to commentary) and the linguistic perspective (from recovered information to degree zero).

§80. This linguistic model has been constructed from a study of modern Western languages and is difficult to apply to Hebrew because that language has much fewer verb forms. In his grammar Schneider was only partially successful. In these notes I have tried to go a stage further but have to acknowledge that some element of doubt remains. In the introduction (§3) I provided a very general picture of the tense system in Hebrew which the following pages make more precise. I will now try to provide a uniform picture using the data obtained.

I must first point out that there do not appear to be any 'temporal metaphors' in Hebrew; there are only tense shifts, as defined above (cf. §94). Besides, the transitions/shifts I am discussing are all heterogeneous (denoted by the symbol →). I am leaving out tense shift from one verbal form to another which is identical (denoted by the symbol ←→). I would say that compared with modern languages, tense shifts are comparatively rare in Hebrew. They occur mostly in the WAYYIQTOL narrative chain (§39) and in speech chains of weQATAL (§§57-59), of volitive forms (§55, 2) and of imperatives (§65). In this way I can concentrate my attention on heterogeneous shifts which usually present more problems. I will not yet attempt to combine the two series (homogeneous and heterogeneous) and so analyse the effect they have on the linguistic nature of texts in the wide sense according to the full method of text linguistics because that would be premature. We need further research on the most difficult points before such a global analysis can be faced. Since they can occur in narrative and in discourse I will examine these two aspects in turn.

a. *Linguistic attitude (narrative/comment, §3.1)*

(1) *In narrative*

§81. We must remember that while Hebrew has only one purely narrative verb form (i.e. for foreground and degree zero), the WAYYIQTOL, it possesses quite a variety of speech forms (§3.1). Only rarely (in the apodosis) can QATAL be used as a narrative form, to indicate degree zero of linguistic perspective (§88). Its normal function is 'retrospective' (§8) 14) and it is therefore linked with the linguistic perspective. Of itself it is indifferent to linguistic attitude occurring as it does in both narrative and speech.

§82. Under 'linguistic attitude' can be classified the rare tense shift WAYYIQTOL → weQATAL or → WAW-x-YIQTOL, both used to denote a repeated action (§46). These shifts also occur with *wayehi* in the following form: *wayehi* + circumstance of time → weQATAL (§35), or → YIQTOL (§34), also to denote a repeated action.

§83. The tense shift WAYYIQTOL → WAW-simple noun clause, which normally belongs to prominence (§86) is classed under linguistic attitude in cases where instead of a single noun clause (circumstance or background to the preceding WAYYIQTOL) a series of simple (and occasionally complex) nominal clauses occurs, descriptive in function. In such texts there is, in fact, an abrupt switch from narrative to comment. We can term them 'comment in the guise of narrative'. We have already come across several examples of this kind in the passages describing preparation of the tent in the desert (Exod. 36.8ff., §58 and Exod. 38, §59). Examples of this kind which are even more varied are 1 Kings 6 (building of the temple) and 7 (building of Solomon's palace). In spite of the many lexical problems in these texts[67] they are still interesting with respect to tense shift. In them we find that narrative, using WAYYIQTOL for listing in turn each stage of the construction as it was carried out, alternates with comment in which different kinds of noun clauses describe each of the stages.[68]

1 Kings 6

1	ויהי בשמונים שנה ....
	ויבן הבית ליהוה
2	והבית אשר בנה המלך שלמה ליהוה
	ששים־אמה ארכו
	ועשרים רחבו
	ושלשים אמה קומתו
3	והאולם על־פני היכל הבית
	עשרים אמה ארכו על־פני רחב הבית
	עשר באמה רחבו על־פני הבית
4	ויעש לבית חלוני שקפים אטמים
5	ויבן על־קיר הבית יציע (qere) סביב ...
	היציע (qere) התחתנה
	חמש באמה רחבה
	והתיכנה
	שש באמה רחבה
	והשלישית
	שבע באמה רחבה
	כי מגרעות נתן לבית סביב ...
7	והבית בהבנתו
	אבן־שלמה מסע נבנה
	ומקבות והגרזן כל־כלי ברזל לא־נשמע בבית בהבנתו
8	פתח הצלע התיכנה אל־כתף הבית הימנית
	ובלולים יעלו על־התיכנה ומן־התיכנה אל־השלשים

1	In the year. . .
	(Solomon) built the temple of Y.
2	The temple which Solomon built for Y.
	60 cubits its length,
	20 cubits its width,
	and 30 cubits its height

3   The ulam which was in front of the hekal of the temple,
      20 cubits was its length compared with the width of the
            temple,
      10 cubits its width compared with the temple.
4   And he made in the temple windows with gratings and
            shutters(?)
5   And he built, against the wall of the temple, a lean-to
            building(?)
6   The smaller building:
      5 cubits was its length;
      The middle (storey?)
      6 cubits was its width;
      the third: 7 cubits was its width, because he had made offsets on
            the temple around. . .
7   The temple, when it was built
      with stone prepared at the quarry was it built
      neither hammers nor chisels nor any other iron
      tool was heard in the temple when it was built.
8   The entrance to the middle storey was on the right side of the
            temple
      and some steps went up to the second storey
      and from the second storey to the third.

This short passage is enough to illustrate the alternation between
narrative and comment which is characteristic of all 1 Kings 6 and 7
also. The different constructions used for comment which occur can
be reduced to two types of noun clause. One is the two-element
simple clause, and is more common. The other is the compound
clause—WAW-noun-finite verb—comprising either QATAL (twice
in v. 7) or YIQTOL (v. 8) for a continuous action.

§84. Similar to the foregoing are cases where the writer arrests the
narrative to provide a commentary of his own on events. This kind of
commentary is longer than a single clause and turns into a narrative
which is then not independent but subsidiary to the comment itself.
In such cases we can speak of 'narrative comment' to distinguish it
from 'comment in the guise of narrative' (§83). In 'narrative
comment' there is, likewise, the tense shift WAYYIQTOL → simple
nominal clause; but then the reflection provided by the writer
becomes, in turn, a narrative. This results in a new shift: simple noun
clause → WAYYIQTOL. In 'comment in the guise of narrative',
instead, there is a repeated alternation between narrative and

comment which gives rise to a series of shifts: WAYYIQTOL
simple (or complex) nominal clause.

2 Kgs 17.34-41 comprises a good example of 'narrative comment'.
After a series of narrative forms (vv. 32-33) the text continues:

2 Kings 17

34	עד היום הזה הם עשים כמשפטים הראשנים
	אינם יראים את־יהוה
	ואינם עשים כחקתם וכמשפטם וכתורה
	וכמצוה אשר <u>צוה</u> יהוה את־בני
	יעקב אשר־שם שמו ישראל
35	<u>ויכרת</u> יהוה אתם ברית
	<u>ויצום</u> לאמר ...
(direct speech)	
40	ולא שמעו
	כי אם־כמשפטם הראשון הם עשים
41	<u>ויהיו</u> הגוים האלה יראים את־יהוה
	ואת־פסליהם <u>היו</u> עברים
	גם־בניהם ובני בניהם כאשר עשו אבתם
	הם עשים עד היום הזה

34 To this day they act in accordance with the ancient customs,
   they do not fear Y.
   and they do not act in accordance with their statutes or their
   ordinances or the law or the commandment which Y. had given
   the sons of Jacob to whom he gave the name of Israel.
35 Indeed, Y. had made a covenant with them
   and had commanded them as follows: (speech)
40 But they did not listen
   instead they act in accordance with their ancient custom.
41 And so those peoples have become reverers of Y.
   but their idols they also worshipped.
   Even their children and their children's children, as their
   fathers had done they also do the same to this day.

The inclusio עד היום הזה הם עשים כשפטים הראשנים (v. 34) עד הם עשים
היום הזה (v. 41) is used in this passage. This literary datum shows that
the whole passage is an editorial comment on the theme of the
Samaritans who were spoken of earlier. In v. 34 the comment uses
the simple noun clause. From v. 35, however, the comment develops
into a narrative which uses WAYYIQTOL and its corresponding
negative ולא + QATAL (v. 40a). This narrative explains the clause
אשר צוה יהוה (with retrospective QATAL, §8); the WAYYIQTOLs,
therefore, acquire the tense of their antecedent.

Verse 40b uses the simple noun clause again, whereas v. 41 goes back to WAYYIQTOL and then shifts to WAW-x-QATAL in order to place emphasis on the subject, as happens both in narrative proper (§48) and in 'narrative discourse' (§77). Verse 41 closes with a simple noun clause.

(2) *In speech*

§85. 'Narrative discourse' originates chiefly from the tense shift (x-) QATAL → WAYYIQTOL (§§74-77) and therefore seems to be a shift from a speech form to a narrative form. In actual fact, though, this WAYYIQTOL is not narrative in character but a continuation form (§§76, 78) and so the shift is only grammatical, not syntactic. Accordingly, in discourse no real shift connected with linguistic attitude occurs.

b. *Prominence (foreground/background)*

(1) *In narrative*

§86. In narrative, the foreground is usually denoted by WAYYIQTOL, by QATAL or by the WAW-x-QATAL construction only in the apodosis of the 'two-element syntactic construction' and by temporal constructions with or without a preceding *wayehi* (§§126, 127). Background is denoted by a simple noun clause.

The tense shift WAYYIQTOL → WAW-x-QATAL (§§9-10) falls under prominence when in one way or another (simultaneity, §41, contrast, §42, emphasis, §48) it marks a shift from foreground to background. I call this construction a background WAW-x-QATAL so as not to confuse it with the WAW-x-QATAL of antecedent where the reverse shift occurs: WAW-x-QATAL → WAYYIQTOL (§15).

Mention must also be made of the shift WAYYIQTOL → WAW-simple noun clause, which marks a contemporaneous circumstance (§43). It will be remembered that I classed this shift under linguistic attitude when the noun clause as here does not represent a simple circumstance of the main action but becomes long and independent ('comment in the guise of narrative', §83). It needs to be noted, though, that the difference between comment (linguistic attitude) and background (prominence) is rather nuanced in Hebrew narrative (cf. §94, type 2).

(2) *In speech*

§87. In speech, foreground is expressed by the indicative x-YIQTOL, volitive forms or the simple noun clause; background by (WAW-) simple noun clause, to express a contemporaneous circumstance or by WAW-x-QATAL for an antecedent circumstance (§51).

For the corresponding tense shifts see §54. Another shift connected with prominence is weQATAL → WAW-x-YIQTOL in order to emphasize the element 'x' (§§58-59).

In 'narrative discourse' the shift WAYYIQTOL → WAW-x-QATAL (foreground → background) occurs as in narrative proper (§§75, 77), as does the shift x-QATAL → simple nominal clause (e.g. Deut 5.2-5, §77) which likewise marks the shift from foreground to background (§94, type 4).

Linguistic perspective (recovered information/degree zero/ anticipated information)

(1) *In narrative*

§88. In narrative, recovered information (retrospection or antecedent action) is expressed by initial WAW-x-QATAL, degree zero by WAYYIQTOL (with QATAL or WAW-x-QATAL only in the two-element syntactic construction with or without a preceding *wayehi*, cf. §§126, 127) and anticipated information by YIQTOL. The following are some examples of this use of YIQTOL in narrative:

Gen. 2.19b

ויבא אל־האדם
לראות מה־יִקְרָא־לו

He (God) brought (the animals) to Adam
to see what he would have called them.

Exod. 2.4

ותתצב אחתו מרחק
לדעה מה־יֵעָשֶׂה לו

His sister stayed at a distance
in order to know what would have happened to him
('what would have been done to him')

2 Kgs 13.14a

ואלישע חלה את־חליו אשר יָמוּת בו

Now Elisha fell sick with the sickness of which (eventually) he would die.

Note that the YIQTOL has a similar prospective function in discourse also (§52).

The tense shift is of the type WAW-x-QATAL → WAYYIQTOL when the antecedent action is a single action in the past (this QATAL sometimes requires translation by the pluperfect in English) or WAW-simple noun clause → WAYYIQTOL to indicate a condition or a continuous action, or by WAW-x-YIQTOL → WAYYIQTOL to indicate a repeated action. On this topic see §§16, 18 (and note 33), 19, 91.

§89. When the antecedent action develops into a short independent narrative, the opening construction is continued by WAYYIQTOL even though the passage retains its character of recovered information; in this case, too, the tense shift is WAW-x-QATAL (or other noun clause) → WAYYIQTOL (§27).

§90. It is worth while examining Job 1.1-5 as it is a lengthy and complex example of an antecedent which develops into a short narrative.

Job

1	אִישׁ הָיָה בְאֶרֶץ־עוּץ אִיּוֹב שְׁמוֹ
	וְהָיָה הָאִישׁ הַהוּא תָּם וְיָשָׁר וִירֵא אֱלֹהִים וְסָר מֵרָע
2	וַיִּוָּלְדוּ לוֹ שִׁבְעָה בָנִים וְשָׁלוֹשׁ בָּנוֹת
3	וַיְהִי מִקְנֵהוּ שִׁבְעַת אַלְפֵי־צֹאן וּשְׁלֹשֶׁת
	אַלְפֵי גְמַלִּים וַחֲמֵשׁ מֵאוֹת צֶמֶד־בָּקָר
	וַחֲמֵשׁ מֵאוֹת אֲתוֹנוֹת וַעֲבֻדָּה רַבָּה מְאֹד
	וַיְהִי וְהָאִישׁ הַהוּא גָּדוֹל מִכָּל־בְּנֵי־קֶדֶם
4	וְהָלְכוּ בָנָיו
	וְעָשׂוּ מִשְׁתֶּה בֵּית אִישׁ יוֹמוֹ
	וְשָׁלְחוּ
	וְקָרְאוּ לִשְׁלֹשֶׁת אַחְיֹתֵיהֶם לֶאֱכֹל וְלִשְׁתּוֹת עִמָּהֶם
5	וַיְהִי כִּי הִקִּיפוּ יְמֵי הַמִּשְׁתֶּה
	וַיִּשְׁלַח אִיּוֹב
	וַיְקַדְּשֵׁם
	וְהִשְׁכִּים בַּבֹּקֶר
	וְהֶעֱלָה עֹלוֹת מִסְפַּר כֻּלָּם
	כִּי אָמַר אִיּוֹב
	אוּלַי חָטְאוּ בָנַי
	וּבֵרְכוּ אֱלֹהִים בִּלְבָבָם
	כָּכָה יַעֲשֶׂה אִיּוֹב כָּל־הַיָּמִים

1   There was a man in the land of Uz called Job.
     This man was upright and just, God-fearing and opposed to
     sin.
2   And to him were born seven sons and three daughters
3   ‍nd his property comprised 7,000 sheep, 3,000 camels, 500 yoke
     of oxen, 500 she-asses and a great number of slaves.
     And so that man was greater than all the sons of the East.
4   And his sons went and banqueted in the house of each (other) in
     turn and they sent invitations ('and they sent and they invited')
     to their three sisters to eat and drink with them.
5   And when they had completed the series of banquets Job sent
     (for them)
     and sanctified them.
     He would get up early
     and offer sacrifices corresponding to their total number.
     For Job thought:
     'Perhaps my children have sinned
     and 'blessed God in their heart'.
     That is what Job used to do each time.

From the literary aspect the passage can be divided into two parts:
vv. 1-3, with the inclusio between v. 1 איש—האיש ההוא and v. 3
האיש ההוא, and vv. 4-5, with the inclusio between יומו of v. 4, ימי at the
beginning of v. 5 and כל־הימים at the end of v. 5. The character is
introduced by the x-QATAL construction since it comprises an
absolute beginning.[65] Each of the two parts then uses the weQATAL
construction for repeated actions. It is evident that repeated actions
are involved from the concluding clause of v. 5 which has x-YIQTOL
(with emphasis on the adverb ככה).

In both parts, then, the transition from weQATAL → WAYYIQTOL
occurs, and so the construction denoting a prior event becomes a
short narrative but remains antecedent in character. In v. 5 weQATAL
then returns to describe the actions which Job repeatedly carried out
and they are explained by כי+QATAL followed by a short direct
quotation. The actual narrative, introduced by *wayehi*, does not
really begin till v. 6. Note that v. 5 also contains a *wayehi* but it
belongs to the antecedent (cf. Gen. 39.5: §91) while the two *wayehi*'s
of v. 3 are two forms of היה as a verb in its own right, not as a macro-
syntactic sign of narrative (§28).

The weQATAL used here in the antecedent for habitual actions is
the same commenting form which occasionally breaks the chain of
narrative WAYYIQTOLs (§§46, 82). Accordingly, the whole passage

is intelligible within the syntactic frame shown. I think Schneider is over-hasty, therefore, when he asserts: 'In later narrative literature (for example, at the beginning of the book of Job) this use of the imperfect with ן has become more widespread in narrative contexts'.[66] Verses 1-5 are not really the actual narrative but its antecedent.

§91. It is noticeable that constructions with an antecedent are quite varied and well differentiated: WAW-x-QATAL is used for a single past action, WAW-simple noun clause for a contemporaneous state (or an action when there is a participle), WAW-x-YIQTOL or weQATAL for a repeated action (cf. §§19, 88). The shift from all these constructions is to the WAYYIQTOL which can be narrative in the strict sense and so comprise the beginning of the narrative, or (it can) continue the antecedent construction in which case not be true narrative. When it comes to actual examples, though, it is not always easy to determine where the antecedent ends and where the narrative begins. An example is provided by the following text.

Genesis 39

1	ויוסף הורד מצרימה
	ויקנהו פוטיפר סריס פרעה שר הטבחים
	איש מצרי מיד הישמעאלים אשר <u>הורדהו</u> שמה
2(a)	ויהי יהוה את־יוסף
(b)	ויהי איש מצליח
(c)	ויהי בבית אדניו המצרי
3(a)	וירא אדניו כי יהוה אתו
(b)	וכל אשר־הוא עשה יהוה מצליח בידו
4(c)	וימצא יוסף חן בעיניו
	וישרת אתו
(d)	ויפקדהו על־ביתו
	וכל־יש־לו נתן בידו
5(d)	ויהי מאז הפקיד אתו
	בביתו ועל כל־אשר יש־לו
	ויברך יהוה את־בית המצרי בגלל יוסף
	ויהי ברכת יהוה בכל־אשר יש־לו בבית ובשדה
6(d)	ויעזב כל־אשר־לו ביד־יוסף
	ולא־ידע אתו מאומה כי אם־הלחם אשר־הוא אוכל
	ויהי יוסף יפה־תאר ויפה מראה

1   Now Joseph had been led to Egypt
     and Potiphar, pharaoh's courtier, the chief of the bakers
     (and) an Egyptian, had bought him from the Ishmaelites
     who had let him there.

2	Y. was with Joseph who became a successful man and entered the house of his master, the Egyptian.[70]
3	His master saw that Y. was with him and that all he did, Yahweh turned to his success.
4	So Joseph was well regarded by him and entered his personal service and to him he entrusted his house and all he possessed he placed under his authority.
5	Now, from the time he entrusted him with his house and with all he possessed, Y. blessed the Egyptian's house on Joseph's account and Y.'s blessing was on everything he possessed in house and field.
6	And so he left all that belonged to him in Joseph's hand and did not demand account for anything except the food he ate. Now Joseph was handsome and good-looking.

The initial WAW-x-QATAL construction of the antecedent (§16) is carried on by a WAYYIQTOL with the same tense value. This is evident from the stylistic repetition הורד מצרימה—הורדהו שמה which forms an inclusion in v. 1. Afterwards, however, the text provides no linguistic clues as to where the antecedent ends and the actual narrative begins. In my opinion, though, both style and meaning indicate that the whole passage is to be understood as antecedent. It hardly gives the impression of narrative, replete as it is with explanatory clauses: compare vv. 2 and 3-4a (the pattern of equivalences is abc—abc), 4b-6a (d—d'—d). Verse 6b provides an item of information connected with the next episode (Joseph's temptation); if it had not already been inserted in the context of the antecedent (event) it would be permissible to expect a construction which was not WAYYIQTOL. I think, therefore, that the *wayehi* of v. 5 must also be interpreted within the frame of antecedent, like the *wayehi* of Job 1.5 (§90). The narrative itself, then, begins with the *wayehi* of v. 7, as in Job 1.6.

§92. In discourse the levels of the linguistic perspective are indicated quite clearly. Retrospective QATAL, usually preceded by כי or אשר, is used for recovered information. Degree zero can be represented by one of the constructions belonging to the three basic time axes: volitive forms or simple noun clauses for the axis of present time, indicative x-YIQTOL for the future, (x-)QATAL for the past. Anticipated information is denoted by the indicative YIQTOL (§52), by indirect volitive forms of purpose, by weQATAL (§61) or by final clauses.

(2) *In discourse/speech*

§93. Narrative discourse (§§74-78) develops the report QATAL (§§22-23) in the normal way, through a series of WAYYIQTOLs. This QATAL differs syntactically from the retrospective QATAL as it is at degree zero (§8, cf. §135, no. 3). Accordingly, in narrative discourse the shift QATAL → WAYYIQTOL does not imply any change linked with the linguistic perspective.

§94. In conclusion, two main types of tense shift occur in narrative:

—type 1: WAYYIQTOL → WAW-x-QATAL, where the transition is from foreground to background (degree of prominence, §86) and WAW-x-QATAL → WAYYIQTOL, where the shift is from antecedent to degree zero (linguistic perspective, §88).

—type 2: WAYYIQTOL → weQATAL / WAW-x-YIQTOL, with a move from the narrative form to commentary form (linguistic attitude, §82), and WAYYIQTOL → WAW-simple noun clause, again with the move from narrative form to commentary form (particularly clear in the case of 'narrative as commentary', §83).

As for the comment forms of type 2 it needs to be said that the tense they have in narrative differs from their tense in discourse. Whereas weQATAL and WAW-x-YIQTOL denote repetition in narrative, in discourse they denote the future (cf. §135, nos. 8-9) and the simple noun clause expresses contemporaneity in narrative but the present in discourse (cf. §135, no. 10). Now, both repetition and contemporaneity belong to the linguistic level of background. For this reason the border between comment (linguistic attitude) and background (prominence) is fluid. This fluidity is reflected in the terminology I have used in the course of the present volume, where comment and background are often considered to be equivalent. On the other hand, this situation indicates that type 2 tense shifts are not twofold ('metaphors') but simple. Even so they are greater with respect to type 1 shifts and signify an abrupt break in the narrative flow.

The tense shifts which occur in discourse can also be reduced to two types:

—type 3: foreground construction → WAW- simple noun clause, or → WAW-x-QATAL, both background constructions (prominence, §87). To the same type (foreground → background) belongs the shift x-QATAL → simple noun clause which occurs in narrative discourse (§87).

—type 4: (x-)QATAL → WAYYIQTOL (narrative discourse, §85), where it only looks as if there has been a change in linguistic attitude. In fact, here the WAYYIQTOL is not narrative but continuative and so does not have its own tense and linguistic level; instead, it takes on those of the preceding form (§146).

Both these types of shift in discourse, then, are minor since they do not involve any transition linked with linguistic attitude.

In conclusion, I think that in Hebrew all the (tense-)shifts are of the first degree and there are no 'temporal metaphors', apart from those cases where there is a transition from narrative to direct speech. In such cases, besides the shift connected with linguistic attitude (narrative → discourse), there can be another shift affecting linguistic perspective; for example, degree zero → anticipated information (as in Josh. 1.16-18, §52). Now, temporal metaphors are absent from true narrative because the biblical author never intrudes in the first person or uses verb forms proper to speech in his narrative, which is not the case in the modern novels examined by Weinrich. Intrusions by biblical writers are more indirect in character and although the verb forms used belong to discourse, in a narrative context their tense changes completely (see type 2, above).

Chapter 8

THE TWO-ELEMENT SYNTACTIC CONSTRUCTION (2SC)
(Protasis-apodosis)

§95. It is true that inter-clausal relationships have not been studied
to any depth in grammars and this applies to both hypotaxis and, in
particular, parataxis (apposition and coordination).[71] This is definitely
a serious problem and merits detailed research in view of its
considerable importance for translating texts and for exegesis. A
comparison between different versions is enough to make one realise
that a main clause in one version is judged to be a secondary clause in
another, and vice versa. In prose it often happens that the
monotonous succession of WAYYIQTOLs forces the translator to
make some of the clauses subordinate in the manner appropriate to
modern languages. But how is it possible to determine which clause
is subordinate to another?

Although the present study does not address this problem directly,
it can still provide wide-reaching suggestions. First of all it should be
noted that the formulation of valid criteria (morphological and
syntactic as well as semantic) for isolating hypotaxis and parataxis,
presents problems. If we consider WAW, for example, it is clearly
'neutral' in the sense that it tells us nothing about the syntactic
character of the connection it creates, whether it is coordinating
(parataxis) or subordinating (hypotaxis). On the other hand, sometimes
the WAW is missing and yet no change results. This is why I put it in
brackets, for example is the constructions (WAW-)x-QATAL or
(WAW-)x-YIQTOL. The syntactic function of such constructions is
unchanged whether WAW is present or not. It is also a problem to
identify hypotaxis whenever there are no explicit markers (e.g.
למען, כאשר, כי, אם etc.) which happens most of the time. For these
reasons, then, it seems to me that here too, there is no chance of
arriving at valid criteria unless we take into consideration not just
the individual clause but the sentence and the longer speech or

narrative unit, according to the methodology of text linguistics. See, for example, the criteria used in §§36, 126, 135.

Now, before it is possible to speak about either parataxis or hypotaxis we have to determine when a clause is independent and when, instead, it is dependent. (I am aware that in the following summary I will repeat material already given but I will also be forced to anticipate the conclusions of several paragraphs yet to come.) In respect of this problem I maintain that the only valid criterion is position within the clause (§135). In general it is true that a clause is independent when the finite verb is in first position but it is dependent when the finite verb is in second position. Rather, to be more precise, the criterion of first or second position can operate at two levels: the level of the individual clause (grammar) or the level of the speech or narrative unit (text linguistics syntax). This means that there are cases in which a clause is independent in terms of grammar (main clause) but dependent in terms of text linguistics (main clause which cannot exist alone in the text). Now, a clause is a main clause when the finite verb form is not preceded by a conjunction, and a main clause can exist in isolation when the finite verb form is initial (i.e., in first position in a unit of narrative or speech). For a clause to be independent, syntactically, the requirement is that both conditions apply: it has to be a main clause and it has to exist on its own.

Applying these criteria we can classify all the verb forms and grammatical constructions of Hebrew into three categories (the numbers refer to Table 2 of §135).

(1) The following initial constructions comprise independent clauses in terms of grammar and of syntax:

- narrative WAYYIQTOL (no. 1)
- direct volitive forms (no. 2)
- the QATAL and x-QATAL of report (no. 3)

(2) The following non-initial constructions are independent in terms of grammar but dependent in terms of syntax;

- the WAYYIQTOL of continuation, including *wayehi* (§135, nos. 11-13 and §146)
- constructions for antecedent and background (nos. 7-10)
- indicative x-YIQTOL(?) (no. 5: see the relevant discussion in §135)
- weQATAL (no. 8)
- the indirect volitive forms (no. 4) when denoting purpose (see the relevant discussion in §135)

(3) Finally, the following non-initial constructions, which are also not principal clauses are dependent in terms of grammar and of syntax:

— conjunction + QATAL (no. 6) or conjunction + YIQTOL (no. 9)
— constructions of the protasis (no. 14), including those preceded by *wayehi* (§127).

Now, corresponding to the three cases of independence/dependence there are three types of parataxis/hypotaxis:

(1a) Grammatical and syntactic parataxis of equal independent constructions:

— chain of narrative WAYYIQTOLs. In this case all the facts are at degree zero (§3, 3), generally in close succession, sometimes closural (§140). Usually there is no justification for changing this state of affairs in translation by making one clause subordinate to another, except in cases of the type ‏וישלח‎. . .‏ויאמר‎. . . 'he sent. . in order to say. . .' (2 Sam. 12.17, §22).
-- chain of imperatives, whether connected by WAW or not (§65)
— chain of cohortatives or jussives connected by WAW (i.e. direct volitive form → indirect volitive form, §61) when meaning indicates they are coordinated not subordinate as purpose clauses (cf. below, 2). Unfortunately I am unable to provide absolute linguistic criteria for distinguishing between these usages (cf. §§64, 135, no. 4).
— chain of coordinated weQATALs (§§57-59). Note, however, that the first weQATAL of the chain is not independent in terms of syntax (see below, 2). Note, also, that there are no chains of 'report' QATALS since for that form the continuation form is a WAYYIQTOL (see below, 1b). The rare examples of continuation weQATALs equivalent to the past tense are problematic (§158 bis).

(1b) Parataxis of different constructions which have the same tense:

— the (x-)QATAL of report → continuation WAYYIQTOL (narrative discourse, §§74ff.)
— antecedent construction → continuation WAYYIQTOL

('short independent narrative', §27). Similarly, too, other cases where the continuation WAYYIQTOL occurs (§146)
— indicative x-YIQTOL → weQATAL (§55.1)

(2) Grammatical parataxis (i.e., with main clauses) which is really syntactic hypotaxis:

— constructions of antecedent and background *vis à vis* narrative WAYYIQTOL (§126.5-6)
— constructions of apodosis *vis à vis* constructions of protasis (§126.2) even when *wayehi* is present (§127.1). In these cases the WAW of apodosis can be omitted.
— weQATAL *vis à vis* the various constructions which precede it (§57)
— *wayehi vis à vis* the preceding narrative form (§127, 2)
— indirect volitive forms when denoting purpose (see 1a, above)

(3) Grammatical and syntactic hypotaxis

— conjunction + QATAL, or conjunction + YIQTOL, when such constructions precede the main clause and so function as the protasis, or when they following the main clause
— other constructions of the protasis, even when *wayehi* is present (cf. 2, above).

In my opinion this provides in outline a complete system of the relationships among clauses which permits analysis not only of single clauses but also of paragraphs and of longer units in discourse or narrative. In addition, this classification, according to the three degrees of parataxis and hypotaxis, is not based on semantic criteria but on grammatical and syntactic criteria.

§96. In order to provide at least a partial study of this problem—inter-clausal relationships—I have chosen the 'two-member syntactic construction' (2SC) which, as we shall see, enables us to classify the different types of clause using a single model. This 'pattern' is usually termed the construction with 'WAW of apodosis'. I prefer more generic terminology, though, because the WAW of apodosis is not always actually present (cf. §122).

For convenience the first element of the 2SC can be called the 'protasis' and the second the 'apodosis' even though they do not refer exclusively to the conditional clause. The list that follows is based for the most part on Beyer.[72] I will classify the different examples according to the type assigned to the first member or 'protasis'. For each type I will provide an example of every variation I have found to occur, whether of protasis or of apodosis. From time to time I shall say whether narrative (N) or discourse (D) is involved.

a. *Classification*

§97. (1) *A conditional clause*

(second element)	(first element)
Gen. 18.26 D	
	אם־אמצא
ונשאתי לכל־המקום בעבורם	בסדם חמשים צדיקם בתוך העיר
If I find, in Sodom and Gomorrah, fifty just men in the city	I shall pardon the whole region on their account.
Exod. 22.11 D	
ישלם לבעליו	ואם גנב יגנב מעמו
And if (the animal) is stolen by him	he will repay (it) to his master.
Exod. 40.37 N	
ולא יסעו עד־יום העלתו	ואם־לא יעלה הענן
And if the cloud did not rise	they would not leave until the day that it did rise
Gen. 44.22b D	
ומת	ועזב את־אביו
If he (Benjamin) should leave his father	he will die.

§98. (2) *Clause of time*

Gen. 31.8 D	
וילדו כל־הצאן נקדים	אם־כה יאמר נקדים יהיה שכרך
וילדו כל־הצאן עקדים	אם־כה יאמר עקדים יהיה שכרך
When he (Laban) said: 'The spotted ones shall be your wages'	all the flock bore spotted ones;
and when he said: 'The striped ones shall be your wages'	all the flock bore striped ones.

Deut. 12.29-30 D

כי־יכרית
יהוה אלהיך את־הגויים אשר אתה
בא־שמה לרשת
אותם מפניך
וירשת אתם
וישבת בארצם

השמר לך
פן־תנקש אחריהם

29 When Y. your God shall destroy
in front of you the peoples whom
you are going to dispossess
when you dispossess them
and live in their land

30 take care
not to be ensnared after them. . .

Exod. 33.8-10 N

יקומו כל־העם
ונצבו איש פתח אהלו
והביטו אחרי משה עד באו האהלה

והיה כצאת משה אל־האהל

ירד עמוד הענן
ועמד פתח האהל
ודבר עם־משה

והיה כבא־משה האהלה

וראה כל־העם את־עמוד הענן
עמד פתח האהל

וקם כל־העם
והשתחוו איש פתח אהלו

8 As soon as Moses came out towards
the tent

all the people would rise
and each would stand at
the entrance to his own tent
and would follow Moses with
their eyes until he reached
the tent.

9 And as soon as Moses reached the
tent

down would come the column of
cloud and would stay at the entrance
to the tent and he (God) would
speak with Moses.

10 And when all the people used
to see the column of cloud stand
at the entrance to the tent

all the people would stand and

they would prostrate themselves,
each at the entrance of his own
tent.

1 Sam. 2.15 N

ובא נער הכהן ואמר

גם בטרם יקטרון את־החלב

Even before the fat burned

the priest's servant came
and said

Exod. 15.19 N

כי בא סוס פרעה ברכבו
ובפרשיו בים

וישב יהוה עליהם את־מי הים

When Pharaoh's horse, with chariots
and riders entered the sea

Y. made the waters of the
sea turn back on them.

§99. (3) *A relative clause or a participle used as a conditional*

Gen. 44.9 D

ומת

אשר ימצא אתו מעבדיך

The one among your servants with
whom it (the cup) is found

shall die.

Gen. 44.10 D

יהיה־לי עבד
ואתם תהיו נקים

אשר ימצא אתו

The one with whom it (the cup) is
found

shall be my slave,
whereas you shall be
innocent.

Exod. 9.20-21 N

הנים את־עבדיו ואת־נמקהו אל־הבתים
ויעזב את־עבדיו ואת־מקנהו בשדה

הירא את־דבר יהוה מעבדי פרעה
ואשר לא־שם לבו אל־דבר יהוה

20 Those among Pharaoh's
servants who revered Y.'s word

made their slaves and
their cattle flee into
the houses;

21 those, instead, who paid no
attention to Y.'s word

abandoned their slaves
and their cattle in the
countryside.

Exod. 12.15b D (cf. 12.19b D)

כי כל־אכל חמץ   ונכרת הנפש ההיא מישראל

For anyone who eats leavened food   he shall be outlawed from Israel.

§100. (4) *Simple noun clause functioning as a clause of time or as a conditional clause*

Gen. 29.9 N

עודנו מדבר עמם   ורחל באה עם־הצאן

While he (Jacob) was still speaking with them   Rachel arrived with the flock.

Gen. 38.25 N

היא מוצאת   והיא שלחה אל־חמיה לאמר

While she (Tamar) was taken outside he sent word to her   father-in-law.

Judg. 6.13 D

בי אדני

ויש יהוה עמנו   ולמה מצאתנו כל־זאת

Ah, my lord, if Y. is with us   why has all this happened to us?

1 Sam. 9.14 N

המה באים בתוך העיר   והנה שמואל יצא לקראתם

While they (Saul and his servant) entered the city   there was Samuel coming out towards them.

1 Sam. 9.27 N

המה יורדים בקצה העיר   ושמואל אמר אל־שאול

While they were going down towards the edge of the city   Samuel said to Saul.

§101. (5) *Causal clause*

Num. 14.24 D

ועבדי כלב

('casus pendens', cf. §104)

עקב היתה רוח אחרת עמו

וימלא אחרי   והביאתיו אל־הארץ אשר־בא שמה

But my servant Caleb,
since a different spirit was with him
and he followed me wholeheartedly I shall let him enter the
    land he entered.

1 Sam. 15.23b D

וימאסך ממלך

Because you rejected Y.'s word he has rejected you from
(being) king.

יען מאסת את־דבר יהוה

1 Kgs 20.28 D

יען אשר אמרו ארם אלהי הרם יהוה
ולא־אלהי עמקים הוא

ונתתי את־כל־ההמון
הגדול הזה בידך
וידעתם כי־אני יהוה

Since Aram has said 'A god of
the hills is Y.; he is not a god
of the plains'

I shall put all this huge crowd into
your hands and you shall
know that I am Y.

§102. (6) *Infinitive plus preposition functioning as clause of time or cause*

1 Sam. 17.55 N

וכראות שאול את־דוד יצא
לקראת הפלשתי

אמר אל־אבנר שר הצבא ...

Now, as soon as Saul saw David he said to Abner, chief
come out against the Philistine

of the army

1 Sam. 17.57 N

וכשוב דוד מהכות את־הפלשתי

ויקח אתו אבנר
ויבאהו לפני שאול
וראש הפלשתי בידו

And as soon as David came back
from killing the Philistine

Abner seized him and led
him in front of Saul
while he (David) had the
Philistine's head in his
hand.

1 Sam. 21.6 D

בצאתי   ויהיו כלי־הנערים קדש

the young men's bodies have   When I have been on campaign
remained pure.

1 Kgs 13.31 D

במותי   וקברתם אתי בקבר אשר
                איש האלהים קבור בו

When I die

you shall bury me in the
grave where the man of God
is buried.

Exod. 40.36 N

ובהעלות הענן מעל המשכן   יסעו בני ישראל בכל מסעיהם
And when the cloud used to rise the Israelites would
above the tent   leave on all their
                journeys

Num. 14.16 D

מבלתי יכלת יהוה להביא
את־העם הזה אל־הארץ אשר־נשבע להם
                וישחטם במדבר
Since Y. was not able to lead this
people to the land he had
promised them   he destroyed them in the
                desert.

Josh. 3.3 D

כראותכם את ארון ברית־יהוה
אלהיכם והכהנים
הלוים נשאים אתו
                ואתם תסעו ממקומכם
                והלכתם אחריו
As soon as you shall see the ark of
the covenant of Y. your God and
that the levitical priests
are carrying it   you too will leave from
                your position
                and will go behind it.

Josh. 3.15-16 N

וכבוא נשאי הארון עד־הירדן
ורגלי הכהנים נשאי הארון
נטבלו בקצה המים
והירדן מלא על־כל גדותיו כל ימי קציר   ויעמדו המים הירדים מלמעלה
קמו נד־אחד הרחק מאד באדם העיר

אשר מצד צרתן
והירדים על ים הערבה ים־המלח
תמו נכרתו
והעם עברו נגד יריחו

15 Now, as soon as the bearers of the ark reach the Jordan and the feet of the priests bearing the ark were immersed to the edge of the water— and the Jordan was full to all its reaches for all the period of the harvest—

16 the water that was coming down from above ceased and stood up like a single column quite a way from Adamah, the city which is beside Zarethan and (the water) which was coming down on the sea of the Arabah, the Dead Sea, ceased and disappeared and the people crossed in front of Jericho.

§103. (7) *Short indications of time*

Gen. 22.4 N

ביום השלישי

וישא אברהם את־עיניו
וירא את־המקום מרחק

On the third day

Abraham raised his eyes and saw the place from a distance.

Exod. 16.6b-7 D

ערב

וידעתם כי יהוה הוציא אתכם
מארץ מצרים

ובקר

וראיתם את־כבוד יהוה

This evening

you shall know that Y. brought you out of the land of Egypt

and tomorrow

you shall see Y.'s glory.

2 Sam. 15.34 D

עבדך אני המלך אהיה עבד אביך
ואני מאז
ועתה

ואני עבדך

I, your servant, O king
was your father's servant,
and (so) I (was) for a long time
('since then');
and now   your servant am I.

For date-formulas in the historical books cf. §§37-38.

§104. (8) 'Casus pendens'

2 Sam. 19.41b N

וכל־עם יהודה   ויעבירו (ketib) את־המלך

And all the people of Judah   made the king cross over (the Jordan).

2 Chron. 22.10 N

ועתליהו אם אחזיהו
ותקם
ותדבר את־כל־זרע
הממלכה לבית יהודה

ראתה כי־מת בנה

// 2 Kgs 11.1

ועתליהו אם אחזיהו   וראתה. . (!?) (ketib)

(cf. §158 bis, 3)

Athaliah, Ahaziah's mother—   when she saw that her son
was dead, she arose and
destroyed all the royal
descendants of the house
of Judah.

1 Sam. 17.24 N

וכל איש ישראל בראותם את־האיש   וינסו מפניו

And all the men of Judah,   fled away from him.
when they saw that man

Gen. 22.24 N

ושמה ראומה   ותלד גם־היא את־טבח

And his concubine, Reuma by
name   she as well bore Tebah.

1 Kgs 12.17 N

ובני ישראל הישבים בערי יהודה   וימלך עליהם רחבעם

Instead, the sons of Israel,
who lived in the cities of Judah   over them Rehoboam reigned.

1 Kgs 15.13 N

וגם את־מעכה אמו   ויסרה מגבירה

// 2 Chron. 15.16

וגם־מעכה אם אסא המלך   הסירה מגבירה

And even Maacah, his mother   he deprived of the rank
of queen mother.

2 Kgs. 16.14 N

ואת המזבח הנחשת אשר לפני יהוה

ויקרב מאת פני הבית
מבין המזבח ומבין בית יהוה

And the bronze altar which was
in front of Y.

he moved from in front of
the temple, from between
the (new) altar and Y.'s temple
and placed it beside the (new)
altar, facing north.

§105. (9) *Compound noun clause* (x-QATAL)

Gen. 44.3-4 N

הבקר אור

והאנשים שלחו המה וחמריהם

הם יצאו את־העיר לא הרחיקו

ויוסף אמר לאשר על־ביתו

When it was daylight

the men (his brothers)
were dismissed, they and
their asses.

When they had left the city but
had not gone far

Joseph said to his steward.

Exod. 10.13b N

הבקר היה

ורוח הקדים נשא את־הארבה

When it was day (the situation
was as follows)

the east wind had brought
the locusts.

b. *Evaluation*

§106.   Evidently, then, different types of clause can be assigned to
the SC2. In modern languages these correspond to conditional (cases
1, 3, 4), temporal (2, 4, 6, 7, 9) and causal (5, 6) clauses. 'Casus
pendens' (case 8) will be discussed separately (§§119ff.). Note the
abbreviations used in the following tables: D = discourse; N =
narrative; CNC = compound noun clause; SNC = simple noun
clause.

(1) *The conditional clause*

§107.   On the basis of the texts discussed the conditional clause can
have the following constructions in the protasis and the apodosis:

case	PROTASIS	APODOSIS
1	אם + YIQTOL (D) weQATAL (D) אם לא + YIQTOL (N) *	weQATAL, YIQTOL, ולא + YIQTOL weQATAL ולא + YIQTOL
3	אשר + YIQTOL (D)) article + participle (D)) article + participle (N) } (לא) rwa + QATAL (N))	weQATAL, YIQTOL, WAW-x-YIQTOL QATAL, WAYYIQTOL
4	WAW-SNC (D)	WAW-x-QATAL

(*) In a positive clause אם+ YIQTOL (protasis), weQATAL or YIQTOL (apodosis) would be expected, as in D.

(2) *The clause of time*

§108.   A clause of time can have:

case	PROTASIS	APODOSIS
2	אם + (x-)YIQTOL (D) כי + YIQTOL (N) טרם + YIQTOL (N) כי + QATAL (N) weQATAL (N)	weQATAL IMPERATIVE weQATAL WAYYIQTOL YIQTOL, weQATAL
4	SNC (with part.) (N)	WAW-x-QATAL והנה + SNC (with part.)
6	prep. + inf. (d) prep. + inf. (N)	⎧ WAYYIQTOL ⎨ weQATAL ⎩ WAW-x-YIQTOL ⎧ QATAL ⎨ WAYYIQTOL ⎨ YIQTOL ⎩ WAW-x-QATAL
7	(WAW-) adverb of time (D) PREP. + NOUN (N)	⎰ weQATAL ⎱ WAW-SNC WAYYIQTOL
9	x-QATAL (= CNC) (N)	WAW-x-QATAL

§109. The biggest variety of constructions is to be found in clauses of time. For example, a sentence with the pattern 'When so-and-so did this and this, then he (so-and-so) did that and that' (N) is expressed in five different ways (first element—second element):

(i) WAW + (x = 'casus pendens' +) inf. with prep. -WAYYIQTOL

1 Sam. 17.24

וכל איש ישראל בראותם את־האיש
וינסו מפניו (§104)

1 Sam. 17.57

וכשוב דוד מהכות את־הפלשתי
ויקח אתו אבנר (§102)

(ii) כי + QATAL + x-WAYYIQTOL:

Exod. 15.19

כי בא סוס פרעה ברכבו ובפרשיו בים
וישב יהוה עליהם את־מי הים (§98)

(iii) WAW + x ('casus pendens') + QATAL—WAYYIQTOL:

2 Chron. 22.10

ועתליהו אם אחזיהו ראתה כי מת בנה
ותקם ותדבר את־כל־זרע הממלכה לבית יהודה (§104)

2 Sam. 10.14

ובני עמון ראו כי־נס ארם
וינסו מפני אבישי (§45)

(iv) x + QATAL -WAW + x + QATAL:

Gen. 44.3

הבקר אור
והאנשים שלחו המה וחמריהם (§105)

(v) Simple noun clause—WAW + x + QATAL, or והנה + simple noun clause:

Gen. 38.25

היא מוצאת
והיא שלחה אל־חמיה לאמר (§100)

1 Sam. 9.14b

המה באים בתוך העיר
והנה שמואל **יצא** לקראתם (§100)

(vi) weQATAL–weQATAL:

Exod. 33.10

וראה כל־העם את־עמוד הענן . . .
וקם כל־העם . . . (§98).

(3) *Causal clause*

§110.   The causal clause can comprise:

case	PROTASIS	APODOSIS
5	conjunction + QATAL (D)	{weQATAL {WAYYIQTOL
6	prep. + inf. (D)	WAYYIQTOL

Remember that the foregoing tables have been compiled using material discussed in §§97-105 so they cannot be complete. Even so they suffice to give a general picture of the possible variation in 2SC.

For 'casus pendens' (case 8, §104) see §119.

(4) *Constructions used in the protasis*

§111.   Viewed vertically (i.e., first all the constructions in the first half then those in the second) the examples examined so far use the following constructions in the protasis:

(1)   אשר/עקב/יען (אשר)+
/אם/כי/(בטרם)
finite verb (cases/examples 1, 2, 3), or
weQATAL (example 1)

(2)   simple or compound noun clause (cases 4, 9) and
'casus pendens' (example 8);

(3)   prep. + inf. (case 6);

(4)   (prep +) noun, or adverb of time (case 7).

§112.   These constructions correspond to those preceded by *wayehi*.
In fact, all the types of §111 are also found preceded by *wayehi*:

(1) conjunction + finite verb (= type (c) of §30):

Exod. 15.19   Job 1.5

כי בא סוס פרעה... ‏   ויהי כי הקיפו ימי המשתה
(98§)... וישב יהוה   וישלח איוב (90§).

(2a) simple nomional clause (= type (d) of §30):

1 Sam. 9.14b   2 Kgs 13.21

המה באים בתוך העיר   ויהי הם קברים איש
(100§)... והנה שומאל יצא   והנה ראו את־הגדוד (32§)

(2b) compound nominal clause (= type (d) of §30):

Gen. 44.4   2 Kgs 20.4

הם יצאו את־העיר לא הרחיקו   ויהי ישעיהו לא יצא העיר התיכנה
(105§)... ויוסף אמר   ודבר־יהוה היה אליו(32§)

Similarly Gen. 24.45 (... אני טרם אכלה לדבר) as against Gen. 24.15
(33§ ... ויהי־הוא טרם כלה לדבר) which are 'narrative discourse'
and narrative respectively of the same event.

(2c) 'casus pendens' (cf. §121):

1 Sam. 2.13b   1 Sam. 10.11

כל־איש זבח זבח   ויהי כל־יודעו ...
(119§)... ובא נער הכהן   ויראו... (121§).

(3) preposition + infinitive (= type (b) of §30):

1 Sam. 17.57   1 Kgs 8.54

וכשוב דוד ...   ויהי ככלות שלמה להתפלל ...
(102§)... ויקח אתו אבנר   קם מלפבי מזבח יהוה (32§)

(4a) preposition + noun (= type (a) of §30):

Gen. 22.4

ביום השלישי
וישא אברהם את־עיניו (§103)

Gen. 40.20

ויהי ביום השלישי . . .
ויעש משתה לכל־עבדיו (§31)

(4b) adverb of time (= type (a) of §30):

Exod. 16.6b-7

ערב
וידעתם . . .
ובקר
וראיתם . . . (§103)

1 Sam. 14.1

ויהי היום
ויאמר יונתן בן־שאול אל־הנער נשא
כליו
Then, one day
Jonathan, son of Saul, said to his
servant, his armour-bearer.
(cf. 1 Sam. 1.4; 2 Kgs 4.8.11.18;
Job 1.6, 13; 2.1).

As far as I can establish ויהי does not occur before אם or (ב)טרם +
finite verb.[73] It probably could occur, though, since והיה (the
morpheme which corresponds to ויהי, §12) is found in front of אם
(Judg. 6.3, §142) and in front of טרם (in a poetic text, Isa. 65.24).
Neither והיה nor ויהי, though, could precede weQATAL (§111.1)
because this verb form always heads the clause (§57). To enable והיה
or ויהי to come first the weQATAL would have to be replaced with a
conjunction + finite verb which is the construction equivalent to
weQATAL in the protasis (§120).

The fact that ויהי sometimes occurs and sometimes does not in
virtually the same constructions means that syntactically it is an
optional marker in narrative (§127). Note, however, that from the
aspect of text linguistics its function remains (§36).

(5) *The constructions used in the apodosis*

§113. The constructions which occur in the apodosis can be
classified according to the three basic axes of time:

(1) to denote the past: WAYYIQTOL in cases 2 (N), 3 (N), 5 (D), 6
(N/D), 7 (N), 8 (N); QATAL in cases 3 (N), 6 (N) and in the date-
formulas of the historical books (§§37-38); WAW-x-QATAL in cases
4 (N/D), 9 (N);

(2) to denote the present: WAW-simple noun clause in case 7 (D);
or, to express simultaneity: והנה + simple noun clause in case 4 (N);
imperative in case 2 (D);

(3) to denote the future: weQATAL in cases 1 (D), 2 (D), 3 (D), 5 (D), 6 (D), 7 (D); YIQTOL in cases 1 (D), 3 (D); WAW-x-YIQTOL in cases 3 (D), 6 (D); or to express repeated action: weQATAL in case 2 (N), YIQTOL in case 6 (N).

For discussion of these constructions see §126.

§114. The tenses assigned above (§113) to the various constructions can be verified by comparing the oppositions evident between the verb forms of the apodosis when the same construction is used in the protasis. For example, in case 5 (§101) WAYYIQTOL is used for a past action in 1 Sam. 15.23 but weQATAL in 1 Kgs 20.28 for an action in the future; similarly, in case 6 (§102) WAYYIQTOL in 1 Sam. 17.57 but weQATAL in 1 Kgs 13.31. Further, in case 3 (§99) the contrast is between QATAL in Exod. 9.20 (past action) on the one hand and weQATAL in Gen. 44.9 or YIQTOL in Gen. 44.10 (actions in the future) on the other. Now, when the same opposition between verb forms recurs in connection with the same tense a sound conclusion can be drawn concerning the function of the tense or constructions involved (cf. §132). Accordingly, it is my opinion that the tenses assigned above to the various verb constructions are based not only on meaning but also on criteria derived from morphology and syntax.

In this connection one text, already quoted in part, is significant. It contains three different verb forms in succession in the same context: weQATAL, QATAL and WAYYIQTOL, the first in the apodosis of a speech, the other two in the apodoses of a narrative. In all three cases the protasis comprises a 'casus pendens' (in the first case, though, the protasis is complex):

Exod. 9.19b D

	כל־האדם והבהמה
	אשר־ימצא בשרה
	ולא יאסף הביתה
<u>ותמו</u>	וירד עלהם הברד

9.20 N

| הניס את־עבדיו | הירא את־דבר יהוה מעברי פרעה |
| ואת־מקנהו אל־הבתים | |

9.21 N

| ויעזב את־עבדיו | ואשר לא־שם לבו אל־דבר יהוה |
| ואת־מקנהו בשרה | |

9.19b D
Every man and beast
who happens to be in the countryside
and has not been brought home
  when the hail falls upon them   shall die.

For vv. 20-21 see §99. In this example the grammatical and semantic contrast between weQATAL (future) on the one hand and QATAL or WAYYIQTOL (§127, 3) (past) on the other is evident.

§115. As already noted for the protasis (§112) the constructions of the apodosis are identical with those used when the protasis is preceded by *wayehi* (§§31-35). See the discussion in §§126 and 127.

§116. Note that in the 2SC, the tense of the constructions in the apodosis is basically the same in both discourse and narrative, except for expressing the present (D) or simultaneity (N and DN)—or the future (D) or a repeated action (N) (§113, numbers 2 and 3 respectively).[74]

§117. As for the constructions for the past which appear in the second element (§113.1) we can note that WAYYIQTOL is replaced by QATAL when the WAW of apodosis does not occur, although there is no obvious difference (similarly in the date formulas in the historical books which are sometimes preceded by *wayehi*, §§31-32, and sometimes not §§37-38). In some cases, however, the function of the x-QATAL construction seems to be to emphasize the 'x' element (cf. §124, 1b).

Exod. 19.1

בחדש השלישי לצאת בני־ישראל מארץ מצרים
ביום הזה באו מדבר סיני

In the third month after the departure of the children of Israel from the land of Egypt,
that (very) day, they arrived in the Sinai desert.

In this passage[75] it is quite evident that the emphasis is placed on the exact date (cf. Gen. 7.11, §38). This is possibly why the sentence is not preceded by a *wayehi* even though it occurs in a similar text (Exod. 12.41, §30). However, there seems to be no emphasis in, for example, Gen. 22.4 ביום השלישי וישא אברהם את־עיניו (§103).

The other construction for the past, WAW-x-QATAL is used when a noun clause, either simple (§100) or compound (§105) occurs in the first element. Though indicative of a degree of preference for one construction over the other it does not constitute a rule. See the complex passage Josh. 3.15-16 (§102) which has the following coordinated constructions in the protasis: WAW-preposition + infinitive, WAW-x-QATAL (twice): and in the apodosis the following coordinated constructions: WAYYIQTOL, QATAL, WAW-x-QATAL (twice).

§118. The future (§113.3) is denoted indifferently by weQATAL or by YIQTOL without the WAW of apodosis. Compare, for example, Gen. 44.9 אשר ימצא אתו מעבדיך ומת with Gen. 44.10 אשר ימצא אתו יהיה־לי עבר (§99).

(6) *'Casus pendens'*

§119. 'Casus pendens' (§104) merits a separate study because it provides the opportunity for elucidating the syntax of the 2SC. We present the relevant data here.

(1) Regarding the first member: the syntactic equivalence of the construction בטרם + finite verb, expressing time, and the 'casus pendens' is evident from a comparison of

1 Sam. 2.15

גם <u>בטרם</u> יקטרון את־החלב
ובא נער הכהן (§98)

with 1 Sam. 2.13b

<u>כל־איש</u> זבח זבח
ובא נער הכהן
Whoever offered a sacrifice,
the priest's servant would come.

Now 'casus pendens' is a nominal construction in extra-position at the head of the clause: literally: 'Concerning the matter: Everyone who offered a sacrifice...'; this analysis is also valid for the construction expressing time, which is adverbial: 'Concerning the matter: Even before they used to burn the fat...'

§120.   With this conclusion the syntax of all the first components of the protasis-apodosis construction can be stated in general terms. From the morphological aspect, in fact, the constructions of the first elements can be traced back to two types: adverbial and nominal. The adverbial constructions comprise:

—adverb (= noun with preposition)[76] (case 7, §103)
—preposition + noun (case 7, §103)
—preposition + infinitive (case 6, §102)
—conjunction + finite verb (cases 1, §97; 1, §98; 5, §101)
—weQATAL (case 1, §97).

The nominal constructions instead comprise:

—noun ('casus pendens') (case 7, §104)
—relative clause (case 3, §99)
—article plus participle (case 3, §99)
—simple noun clause (case 4, §100)
—compound noun clause (x-QATAL and x-YIQTOL) (case 9, §105).

Now, since in the protasis adverbial and nominal constructions are equivalent (§119) the conclusion has to be that all first members of the 2SC must be analysed as 'casus pendens' or as extra-positional constructions. Further on we shall see that all these constructions, adverbial as well as nominal, correspond to expressions of time with or without a preceding *wayehi* and that they, too, are extra-postional constructions (§127).

For discussion of the syntactic force of constructions of the protasis with finite verb forms see §135.14.

§121.   (2) The equivalence of adverbial and nominal constructions of the first member of the 2SC (sn.119) is also confirmed in that both can be preceded by *wayehi*. In this connection the following example is particularly clear since in it the *wayehi* introduces two circumstances, the first adverbial (preposition + infinitive), the second nominal (simple nominal clause):

Josh. 10.11a

ויהי בְּנֻסָם מִפְּנֵי יִשְׂרָאֵל
הֵם בְּמוֹרַד בֵּית־חוֹרֹן
וַיהוה הִשְׁלִיךְ עֲלֵיהֶם אֲבָנִים גְּדֹלוֹת מִן־הַשָּׁמַיִם עַד־עֲזֵקָה
וַיָּמֻתוּ

And while they (the Amorites) were fleeing from Israel, while they
were on the descent of Beth-Horon,
Yahweh hurled upon them great stones from the sky, up to
Azeqah,
and they died.

Even though not listed under §30, 'casus pendens', too, can be
introduced by *wayehi*:

1 Sam. 10.11

ויהי כל־יודעו מאתמול שלשום ויראו
והנה עם־נבאים נבא

Now all those who had known him (Saul) previously saw: and
there he was prophesying with the prophets.

2 Sam. 2.23b

ויהי כל־הבא אל־המקום אשר־נפל שם עשהאל וימת
ויעמדו

Now all those who had come to the place where Asael had fallen
and had died remained standing.

§122.   (3) For the most part the use of WAW of apodosis in the 2SC
is optional; Beyer[77] observes that it is required after a noun clause
expressing time in the first member (§100, above). Compare, for
example, 1 Kgs 15.13 וגם את־מעכה אמו/ויסרה מגבירה with its parallel 2
Chron. 15.16 וגם־מעכה אם אסא המלך/הסירה מגבירה (§104). The syntactic
structure of 1 Kgs 15.13, which definitely has 'casus pendens' in the
first member, indicates that 2 Chron. 15.16 should be analysed as
'casus pendens' + apodosis without WAW (QATAL).

If this is so, however, then the construction in 2 Chron. 15.16
becomes outwardly identical with the compound noun clause with
QATAL, and often there are no clear indicators for distinguishing
one from the other (§124). In view of its outward similarity with the
compound noun clause some authors reject 'casus pendens' as a valid
syntactic category.[78] In my opinion, though, this conclusion is not
justified. On the contrary, the list of nominal constructions provided
above (§120) shows that 'casus pendens' on its own, without its
apodosis, is equivalent to the complex noun clause. For instance, the
'casus pendens' ובקר of Exod. 16.7 (§103) is the syntactical equivalent
of the compound noun clause הבקר אור of Gen. 44.3 (§105) since each

is the first element of the syntactic construction with protasis-apodosis. I think therefore that 'casus pendens' should be an acknowledged part of Hebrew syntax.

(7) *The construction with 'casus pendens'*
clause and the compound noun

§123.   In spite of outward similarity, the construction with 'casus pendens' and the compound noun clause are different in syntactic structure and in function. 'Casus pendens' is a noun or noun equivalent (§120) freed from the position it would occupy within a normal clause and placed at the head of the sentence. It does not really occupy the first position of the clause but is placed outside it ('extra-position') and reference to it is usually made by an anaphoric or resumptive pronoun. Its function is not to place the emphasis on the nominal part of the sentence now placed at the beginning[79] but to mark off the topic to be considered. If we take 1 Kgs 12.17 (§104) as an example, a normal sentence would run: 'Instead, Rehoboam ruled over the Israelites who dwelt in the cities of Judah'; whereas, the construction with 'casus pendens' becomes 'Instead (as for the) Israelites who lived in the cities of Judah ('casus pendens'). Rehoboam ruled over them (resumptive pronoun)'.

On the other hand, a noun introducing a compound noun clause is actually in first position in the sentence and the emphasis of the whole falls on it. The function of such a clause is to identify the subject (who in fact is performing the action[s]: §6). See full discussion in §126.

§124.   In individual cases it is difficult to decide when 'casus pendens' + apodosis without WAW (QATAL) is involved and when it is a compound noun clause instead, if reliable criteria such as type of construction or meaning are missing. Despite this, if we collect together the data scattered throughout the present investigation we can state that 'casus pendens' can be clearly identified when either of the following two basic syntactic structures is present:

(1) noun (= noun or adverb)   x – finite verb or article + participle

(2) protasis   apodosis

(1) The following constructions belong to the first structure:

(1a) noun (= 'casus pendens')	independent personal pronoun—article + participle
noun (= 'casus pendens')	independent personal pronoun—אשׁר + QATAL
noun (= 'casus pendens')	independent personal pronoun—QATAL
noun (= 'casus pendens')	independent personal pronoun—YIQTOL

For example:

Gen. 24.7

(§6.1) הוּא ישׁלח . . . יהוה אלהי השׁמים . . .

| (1b) noun (= 'casus pendens') | resumption of noun—QATAL |

For example:

Exod. 19.1

(§117) ביום הזה באו . . .   בחרשׁ השׁלישׁי . . .

Exodus 35

בידיה טוו . . .   וכל־אשׁה חכמת־לב
וכל־הנשׁים אשׁר נשׂא לבן אתנה בחכמה טוו את־העזים

| 25a | And every woman who had ability | spun with her hands... |
| 26 | But all the women whose 'heart' moved them in skill— | (they were the ones who) spun the goats' hair |

In Exod. 35.25a וכל־אשׁה חכמת־לב is 'casus pendens' because it is continued by בידיה טוו (x-QATAL); the emphasis falls on בידיה. The pronominal suffix which resumes the initial noun proves that this is a 'casus pendens' (§123). Exod. 35.26, instead is probably a compound nominal clause with the emphasis on the initial noun. It seems, therefore, that spinning goat hair was considered a particularly difficult task, difficult enough to demand a special skill!

(2) The following constructions belong to the second syntactic structure:

(2a) the two-member syntactic construction (§126.2):

| first member = protasis | second member = apodosis |

(2b) *wayehi* + noun ('circum-   'apodosis' (§127)
stance')
(2c) date-formula   'apodosis' (§127)

Note that in the historical books the date-formula occurs with a preceding *wayehi* (construction 2b) and without (construction 2c), mostly with no apparent difference (cf. §38). Sometimes, though, there is reason to conclude that the date is not a 'casus pendens' but the first member ('x') of a compound nominal clause x-QATAL (cf. Gen. 7.11, §38; Exod. 19.1, §117). It should also be noted that in such cases the *wayehi* is missing. This means that one function of *wayehi* is to indicate the following noun (or circumstance) to be in extraposition ('casus pendens'), not the first member of a compound nominal clause. It does not necessarily follow, however, that this is the function peculiar to *wayehi* (on which see §127) as the date-formula can be a 'casus pendens' even in its absence.[80]

§125.   Another indication for identifying 'casus pendens' is the resumption of the initial noun by another noun acting as the subject of the QATAL:

Exod. 35.29

כל־איש ואשה אשר נדב לבם אתם להביא
לכל־המלאכה אשר צוה יהוה לעשות ביד־משה
הביאו <u>בני־ישראל</u> נדבה ליהוה

Every man and woman whose heart urged them to contribute by bringing (something) for all the work which Y. had commanded to be done through M.
the children of Israel brought a contribution to Y.

In this example the detailed and lengthy 'casus pendens' is resumed after the verb and summarized by a new noun: בני־ישראל. As for the syntactic structure this example is similar to the construction 1b of §124, with the difference that the apodosis is of the type QATAL-x- instead of x-QATAL.

There are, then, at least two types of construction which indicate a 'casus pendens' clearly: (1) noun / x-QATAL (where 'x' is an independent personal pronoun or a noun with a resumptive pronominal suffix), and the variant noun / QATAL-x (where 'x' is the subject of the verb); (2) the two-member syntactic construction (protasis / apodosis).

(8) *The two-member syntactic construction (2SC) in detail*

§126. In addition to those already discussed the 2SC—with and without *wayehi* (§§28-36; 37-38 respectively)—there, is yet another way in which syntax can be used to express a circumstance prior to the principal action, except that it is not confined to narrative but is also used in discourse. To understand the syntactic 'state' of the verb forms and grammatical constructions which occur in the second member of the 2SC we need to go back to the list of §113.[81] The following table is based on that paragraph:

		Narrative (N)	Discourse (D)
past		WAYYIQTOL QATAL WAW-x-QATAL	WAYYIQTOL WAW-x-QATAL
present		והנה + SNC	WAW + SNC imperative
future		weQATAL YIQTOL	weQATAL YIQTOL WAW-x-YIQTOL
NB: SNC = simple nominal clause			

(1) On the 'past' axis the N—D distinction disappears (linguistic attitude). The WAYYIQTOL, in fact, occurs as an 'initial form' (because the first member is equivalent to a 'casus pendens' and so extra-positional, §§119-120) not only in N, where this is normal even outside the 2SC (§8) but also in D where it is excluded (§§24, 76). The distinction between recovered information—degree zero (linguistic perspective) and foreground—background (emphasis) also disappears since WAYYIQTOL, QATAL and WAW-x-QATAL are all markers of foreground and degree zero (§127.3.). I have no examples of QATAL in the apodosis but in my opinion it is a possibility.

On the 'present' and 'future' axes there are no anomalies in respect of linguistic attitude since all the forms are used in the same way even outside the 2SC. The SNC occurs in both N and D as does the weQATAL; the imperative occurs only in D. The distinction foreground—background (emphasis) is also maintained, as it also is outside 2SC. The SNC in D is equivalent to the present (foreground) whereas in N it is equivalent to contemporaneous action (background); in the same way weQATAL in D expresses the future (foreground) while in N it expresses repetition (background).

(2) The decisive element to be considered in order to understand the syntactic 'state' of the forms and constructions of the apodosis is that some of them are clearly non-initial outside the 2SC. We have already remarked on the case of WAYYIQTOL in D (1) above. The same is true of QATAL in N (§15), weQATAL (§57) and of YIQTOL (§55.1) in both D and N. Also, WAW-x-QATAL can be initial, it is true, but it denotes neither degree zero (as in the 2SC) nor the foreground but the antecedent (§16). Even the SNC (with or without a preceding הנה) can be initial but is not normally preceded by WAW (see the examples in §§68-69). It is now safe to say that the only verb form which could be initial—the WAYYIQTOL of N in the apodosis of a SNC—never actually occurs in that position.

This means that in the 2SC, even though grammatically the first member is in extra-position ('casus pendens', §§119-120), from the aspect of syntax it comprises the protasis. Accordingly, all the various forms of the apodosis have to be constructions with second position in a period. The apodosis, therefore, comprises the main sentence of the paragraph but it is not syntactically independent because it could not exist without the protasis (syntactic hypotaxis, §95, type 2). If, therefore, we denote the protasis with an 'x' we can tabulate all the types listed in fig. 1 as follows:

> x   WAYYIQTOL
> WAW-x-QATAL
> QATAL
> WAW-(הנה +) SNC
> weQATAL
> YIQTOL
> WAW-x-YIQTOL
> imperative

(3) From this table we can draw an important conclusion which permits a clear distinction to be made between the 2SC and the complex nominal clause (CNC) and confirms what has been said above on this topic (§§122-123). In the 2SC the element 'x' (protasis) is separated grammatically from the following sentence (clause) (apodosis) both when the WAW of apdosis is used and when it is not (§122). In other words, the element 'x' comes first in the paragraph not in the individual clause, as in the following table: (1)

x	continuation WAYYIQTOL WAW-x-QATAL QATAL etc.
first position = protasis	second position = apodosis
single paragraph = 2SC	

In the CNC, though, the element 'x' (or WAW-x) comes first in the individual clause and so receives the emphasis (§6.1): (2)

(WAW-)x-QATAL (WAW-)x-YIQTOL
single sentence = CNC

(4) At this juncture the anomaly already remarked on (§6.2) can be explained: in certain cases the CNC puts no emphasis at all on the element 'x' which precedes the finite verb. Now we have seen that in the 2SC the CNC can occur in the protasis (§111). In this way (for example in the form x-QATAL) it becomes the element 'x' of the 2SC, i.e.:

(x-QATAL) = x first position = protasis	. . . second position = apodosis
single paragraph—2SC	

The result in this case is tension between the emphatic function carried by the element 'x' within the CNC (x-QATAL) and the function of protasis which the very same CNC, taken as a unit, has to exercise as element 'x' of the 2SC (paragraph). This second function, which is wider, has priority. The CNC becomes a nominal construction in extra-position ('casus pendens', §119) and so any hint of emphasis within the individual clause vanishes (cf. §167).

(5) The explanation for the CNC not bearing any emphasis when it is an antecedent construction (§§16ff.) is possible along the same lines. The relationship binding the antecedent constructions (WAW-) x-QATAL or (WAW-)x-YIQTOL to the WAYYIQTOL narrative

form can be described on the analogy of the relationship binding the
protasis and the apodosis of the 2SC (syntactic hypotaxis, §95, type
2) the difference being that the relationship involves a longer
linguistic unit ('narrative unit', §36) not the paragraph, as is
apparent from the following table:

(3)

(WAW-)x-QATAL (WAW-)x-YIQTOL	narrative WAYYIQTOL
antecedent	degree zero
narrative unit	

Another difference from the 2SC is twofold. On the one hand the
antecedent construction, unlike the protasis, is a main sentence
(§19); and on the other, the following narrative WAYYIQTOL is an
independent sentence while the apodosis is the main but not
independent (cf. 2, above) sentence. Note, however, that within the
narrative unit antecedent and degree zero are interdependent,
though to different degrees. Although an antecedent construction is
independent from the point of view of grammar it cannot exist
without the narrative form of degree zero (syntactic dependence,
§95, type 2). And the other way round too: the narrative would be
unintelligible or incomplete without its antecedent (semantic dependence), but could exist on its own (syntactic independence).

(6) Similar reasoning holds for the background constructions
WAW-x-QATAL and WAW-x-YIQTOL (cf. §§39ff.) even though
their relationship with the narrative form is the direct opposite of the
relationship between antecedent and degree zero (narrative form) (cf.
§15):

(4)

narrative WAYYIQTOL	WAW-x-QATAL WAW-x-YIQTOL weQATAL
foreground	background
narrative unit	

No background construction can exist without a foreground form (syntactic hypotaxis, §95, type 2) and vice versa, the foreground form is incomplete without the background construction in the context of the narrative (semantic dependence).

We can conclude that the four syntactic structures examined above can be reduced to two basic types:

—*type a*: with the circumstance (noun, adverb or their equivalents) before the main verb, comprising:

(1)   2SC: x / WAYYIQTOL, etc. The (clause of) circumstance acts as the first member of a sentence made up of protasis / apodosis.

(2)   CNC: x-QATAL, etc. The (clause of) circumstance acts as the first member of the individual sentence and has the emphasis.

(3)   Narrative unit with: antecedent (e.g. WAW-x-QATAL) / degree zero (WAYYIQTOL). Both the circumstance (antecedent) and the narrative form (degree zero) are main clauses but mutually dependent. The CNC which functions as an antecedent is not emphatic at all.

—*type b*: with the circumstance after the main verb comprises:

(4)   Narrative unit with: foreground (WAYYIQTOL) / background (e.g. WAW-x-QATAL). The circumstance (background) does not comprise an independent sentence without the narrative form but even that is incomplete without the circumstance within the narrative unit.

Now the three structures of *type a* can be reduced to one CNC (circumstance + finite verb) and the structure of *type b* is equivalent to a verb clause + circumstance.

We can see, then, that the grammatical, syntactic and linguistic criteria are interwoven and interdependent as one moves gradually from a small unit to a larger unit, or from the single clause to the paragraph (2SC) and eventually to the narrative unit. In all three cases the syntactic link seen to exist between circumstance and main verb is basically dependent on the criterion of 'first position in the sentence' (§135), if the term 'sentence' is understood in the wide sense to include an extended narrative unit as well. At this point I trust that the truth of a statement by Weinrich, quoted previously (cf.

§2, above), can now be appreciated better: 'A grammar which does not accept units beyond the sentence can never perceive, let alone solve the most interesting problems of linguistics'.

§127.   At this stage we also need to discuss the constructions of time examined above: those preceded by *wayehi* (§§28-36) and those that are not (§37). Both of these types are made up of two members: a circumstance of time and a main clause.

In the first type the circumstance of time which follows a *wayehi* can belong to the category of nouns or to the category of adverbs (cf. §30). To the category of nouns belong:

— the participle;
— the relative clause;
— the simple nominal clause;
— the compound nominal clause;

to the category of adverbs belong:

— adverbs of time
— preposition + noun
— preposition + infinitive
— כאשר/כי + finite verb.

One of the following forms or constructions can occur in the main clause:

— WAYYIQTOL
— QATAL
— WAW-x-QATAL (compound nominal clause)
— WAW-simple nominal clause

In the second type the circumstance of time comprises the date-formula (chiefly 'in the year x', category: adverb) while the main clause is marked by one of the following verb forms (§37):

— QATAL
— WAYYIQTOL

The only example I know of WAW-x-QATAL in the main clause, after ביום + infinitive as a circumstance of time (Ruth 4.5) is difficult to understand and is generally corrected by scholars.

(1) Now the syntax of these two types of construction is complex for two reasons. First, because both use practically the same verb forms in the main clause. In the second type (historical date-formula)

it is evident that forms which refer to the time-axes of the present (WAW-simple nominal clause) and of the future (YIQTOL and weQATAL) do not occur. Second, because in the main clause (which in both cases belongs to narrative) QATAL and WAYYIQTOL are interchangeable.

The second reason cannot fail to bring to mind the structure of the two-member syntactic construction (2SC). In it the first member (the protasis) is made up of constructions which are either nominal or adverbial (§120). This means they are equivalent to (and for the most part identical with) constructions expressing a circumstance of time in the preceding two cases (with or without *wayehi*). Besides that, the same verb forms and constructions occur in the second member of the 2SC (the apodosis) with the exception of the imperative (§126, fig. 1).

The inescapable conclusion is that the two constructions (with or without *wayehi*) are equivalent to each other (cf. §112) and that both are equivalent to the 2SC as well. In other words, in a single sentence the circumstance of time comprises the protasis and the main clause the apodosis. The overall identity of these respective constructions in the first and second members proves this in a general way. More specifically, though, decisive proof comes from cases where a QATAL, a YIQTOL or a weQATAL occurs in the second member. Note the QATAL in the second member of each of the following examples:

(§32) ויהי בשנת . . . מֶלֶךְ חזקי . . .2 Kgs 18.1 (1)

(§37) ובשנת . . . מֶלֶךְ אבים . . .1 Kgs 15.1 (2)

(§99) הירא את־דבר יהוה . . .הֵנִיס את־עבדיו . . .Exod. 9.20 (3)

There are no special problems in example (2). The conclusion simply has to be that the date-formula occupying first position in the sentence is 'casus pendens' exactly as in the first member of (3). It may be more difficult, though, to accept the same conclusion for example (1) due to the presence of *wayehi*. It remains true, however, that the syntactic connection מלך—ויהי would be impossible if *wayehi* were a narrative WAYYIQTOL. This impossibility is even more evident in a sentence of the following type:

(4) Exod. 12.41

ויהי מקץ שלשים שנה וארבע מאות שנה
ויהי בעצם היום הזה
(§30) יצאו כל־צבאות יהוה מארץ מצרים

In this example, as in (1), I know of no syntactic construction which allows the two *wayehis* to be analysed as normal WAYYIQTOLs. On the other hand a sentence does occur without a *wayehi* with a structure similar to that of example (4):

Exod. 19.1

בחדש השלישי לצאת בני־ישראל מארץ מצרים
ביום הזה
באו מדבר סיני (§117)

Consider, too, the following examples with YIQTOL or WAYYIQTOL in the second member:

(5) 1 Kgs 14.28

ויהי מדי בא המלך בית יהוה
ישאום הרצים . . . (§34)

(6) 2 Kgs 12.10b

בבוא־איש בית יהוה
ונתנו־שמה . . . את־כל־הכסף המובא בית־יהוה (§35)

Now, on the one hand, in (5) the sequence ויהי—ישאון is completely different from the tense shift WAYYIQTOL—weQATAL—WAW-x-YIQTOL. An example of such a shift occurs in the following passage where weQATAL and WAW-x-YIQTOL provide detail (background) for the main action:

Exod. 18.25-26

ויבחר משה אנשי־חיל מכל־ישראל
ויתן אתם ראשים על־העם . . .
ושפטו את־העם בכל־עת
את־הדבר הקשה יביאון אל־משה
וכל־הדבר הקטן ישפוטו הם (§36)

On the other hand, *wayehi* is missing in (6) even though its structure is like (5).

(2) All this means that the construction *wayehi* + circumstance of time does not comprise an independent clause. The *wayehi* does not agree with the 'subject' of the sentence (when it introduces a noun or a simple or compound nominal clause) and in addition its presence does not change the syntactic structure of the whole in any way. Note

that this conclusion is valid only when *wayehi* is a 'macrosyntactic marker' of narrative (§28) and not when it is a form of the verb היה used in its own right (cf. §36. In the first case, in fact, *wayehi* always occurs together with another clause (the 'apodosis') on which it depends.[82] whereas in the second case it can stand on its own.[83] For example, Job 1.5 does *not* comprise a complete sentence:

ויהי כי הקיפו ימי המשתה (. . .) (§90)

whereas Job 1.3b is a complete, independent sentence:

ויהי האיש ההוא גדול מכל־בני־קדם (§90)

In some grammars, therefore, *wayehi* functioning as a macrosyntactic marker is considered to be a 'fossilized' form of WAYYIQTOL or a simple 'indicator of time'.[81]

In my opinion, to understand the syntactic 'state' of *wayehi*, two basic facts need to be kept in mind. First, that it has no function at all in the single sentence, as stated above; second, that it has a macrosyntactic function within an independent narrative unit where it never comes in first position. Its function, in fact, is to continue the main narrative thread forming a connection with circumstances and events which would otherwise be left hanging (§36). These two facts explain why *wayehi* has no verb function in the individual sentence and as a result does not act like a normal WAYYIQTOL (in contrast with the *wayehi* which is an actual verb). We still have to explain why the *wayehi* has the macrosyntactic function of connecting circumstances and events with the main narrative thread.

Before being able to answer this question two other facts need to be brought into the discussion. *Wayehi* is in second position with the function of continuing not only the actual narrative, where a WAYYIQTOL is in first position, but also an antecedent which has become a 'short independent narrative' (cf. Job 1.5, §90; Gen. 39.5, §91) or even a narrative discourse (e.g. Gen. 44.24, §78; cf. Deut. 2.16; 5.23(2); 9.11) with a non-WAYYIQTOL verb form in first position. Now the tense of *wayehi* changes from instance to instance and corresponds to the verb form which precedes it. In other words, as it is a second position WAYYIQTOL the *wayehi* has no tense of its own, taking on, instead, the tense of its context.

At this point the solution to the problem posed earlier seems clear to me: *wayehi* is in fact a form of the continuation (non-narrative) WAYYIQTOL (§146). This explains its function at text (or independent narrative unit) level. It connects (a circumstance and) an event to the main narrative thread (degree zero) when it continues a narrative WAYYIQTOL; but it can also continue a secondary line of narrative, in other words an antecedent construction. The only difference from a normal continuation WAYYIQTOL is that *wayehi* assumes its verb function not at sentence level but at the level of the narrative unit. Its 'subject', therefore, is not the nominal element of the single sentence (usually missing in any case since *wayehi* is mostly followed by an adverbial element) but the complete paragraph it introduces. This difference can be shown as follows:

Job 1.3 (§90)

ויהי האיש ההוא גדול מכל־בני־קדם

verb + subject (noun)

verb clause

Job 1.5

ויהי + כי הקיפו ימי המשתה
... וישלח איוב

verb + 'subject' (paragraph)

wayehi + two-member syntactic construction (§126)

That is, *wayehi* turns the 2SC into a 'verb clause' which is really nominal and as a result links it with the narrative line of degree zero although in reality the syntactic construction remains unconnected.

In conclusion, *wayehi* is not a 'fossilized' form but a continuation WAYYIQTOL functioning at narrative unit level. Besides, it is not even correct that היה is an 'empty' verb and this applies to both types of *wayehi*. The LXX translation, for example (καὶ ἐγένετο or ἐγένετο δε, is a literal rendering of the force of *wayehi*. Unlike Hebrew, though, modern languages do not need to use a special morpheme to show that a sentence which begins with a circumstantial expression belongs to the main narrative. Accordingly the effect of a mechanical translation such as 'and it happened. . . ' is normally pedantic. Even so it is necessary to make the effort and find, in each individual case, the best way of making explicit the linkage at the level of text which is the essential function of *wayehi*. This is what I have tried to achieve in translating the examples quoted (cf. §§31ff.).

(3) If the foregoing syntactic evaluation is correct then the constructions expressing time, with or without *wayehi* ((1), above)

must be assessed using the results obtained in respect of the 2SC (cf. §§117, 126). In effect, every construction preceded by *wayehi* as well as some without *wayehi* which on the grounds of grammatical structure and of context are not emphatic (§124) are syntactically equivalent to a construction with 'casus pendens'. Those without *wayehi* which instead are emphatic are compound nominal clauses (§123).

As a result, for cases of QATAL and WAW-x-QATAL in the 'apodosis' of constructions with or without *wayehi* (§§32, 37) the discussion concerning these same constructions occurring in the second member of the syntactic construction (§126) holds good. Compare, for example,

2 Kgs 20.4

ויהי ישעיהו לא יצא העיר . . .

ודבר־יהוה היה אליו

and Isa. 38.4 (without the initial circumstance) (§32)

ויהי דבר־יהוה אל־ישעיהו

In consequence the WAW-x-QATAL construction in the 'apodosis' (2 Kgs 20.4) expresses degree zero of narrative in precisely the same way as the WAYYIQTOL (Isa. 38.4). Furthermore, the WAYYIQTOL and the QATAL in the 'apodosis' occur side by side in two completely parallel clauses:

Exod. 16.13

ויהי בערב

ותעל השלו ותכם את־המחנה

ובבקר

היתה שכבת הטל סביב למחנה

    Now in the evening
    up went the quails and covered the camp,
    and in the morning
    there was a layer of dew around the camp.

Altogether different is the case of

Gen. 41.13a

ויהי כאשר פתר־לנו

כן היה

    Now as he (Joseph) had explained to us
    precisely so did it turn out

where x-QATAL in the 'apodosis' is a construction with the emphasis placed on the element preceding QATAL as sometimes happens in the two-member syntactic construction (§124).

Chapter 9

SUMMARY ON THE USE OF TENSE IN PROSE

a. *Criteria*

§128. Before we can summarize the use of tense in prose we need to
set out certain criteria (in addition to those of §§2-5) which have
guided our analysis so far. Strictly speaking this should have been
done at the beginning of the essay, not at the end. It is my belief,
though, that the explanation itself is lucid enough on its own even if
the fundamental criteria were not set out right at the beginning but
instead shown at work in the analysis of texts. In any case at this
stage they should turn out to be more easily understood.

(1) *Morphology and meaning*

§129. The function of a verb form or of a grammatical construction
is dependent on its morphology and on its meaning. Context, style
and literary composition have also to be taken into account since
they combine to determine the meaning of a text.

Quite opportunely Schneider's grammar has shown that the
criterion for analysis is not the value of Hebrew verb forms derived
from translation into modern languages. Nor is it an interpretation of
these forms along psychological and philosophical lines based on the
author's intent, as commonly attempted in the past. Instead, analysis
is determined by morphology and syntax. However, I think Talstra[85]
is right in maintaining the need for placing more value on semantics
than Schneider does, even if it takes second place to morphology and
syntax. This is what I have attempted in the explanation provided
above.

(2) *The synchronic level*

§130.   Verb forms will not be analysed individually in terms of the tense they assume when 'naked' or preceded by WAW as is the case in traditional (classical) grammars. Verb forms without WAW cannot be analysed independently of those preceded by WAW. The tense of a verb cannot be determined from analysis of its form with and without WAW as if these were two entirely separate categories.

Of course, no account can be taken of the diachronic aspect which envisages whether it is possible—and if so, how—to derive forms with WAW from 'naked' forms within the system of Semitic tenses as a whole. Since this problem remains unresolved (cf. §1) the present study must be based on linguistic criteria. In any case, even if the problem had been solved the need for checking whether in practice the use of verb forms at the synchronic level corresponds to their origin as established diachronically would remain.

(3) *'Verb forms' and 'grammatical constructions'*

§131.   The terminology I use, namely, 'verb forms' and 'grammatical constructions', requires a word of explanation. By 'verb forms' I mean the simplest grammatical morphemes which can come at the head of a clause, such as the narrative WAYYIQTOL, the QATAL of reports (§§23-24) the jussive YIQTOL and the weQATAL of speech. By 'grammatical constructions', instead, I mean the various combinations which verbal or nominal forms take on in texts, such as WAW-x-QATAL, WAW-x-YIQTOL, WAW-simple noun clause. 'Grammatical constructions' ᵈ not normally fill the first slot in a clause and, from the aspect of sy. ax can be reduced to the formula WAW + simple or compound noun clause (§6). See the fuller discussion in §135.

(4) *The function of such forms and constructions*

§132.   A verb form or a grammatical construction is a self-contained linguistic category when it can be identified by its grammatical structure and its meaning in contrast with other forms or constructions with different structure and meaning. In this way grammatical structure and corresponding meaning define the linguistic function of a form or construction.[86]

It is clear, then, that the tense of an individual form and construction and therefore the most suitable tense for translation into modern languages is not tied to that actual form or construction but to its function in the text. Accordingly, a list of the different functions which an individual form or construction can have in different contexts can be drawn up only after analysis of the individual forms and constructions within the linguistic context.

(5) *Tense and 'mode of action'*

§133. We have already stated that semantics is of importance, even if only secondary, in determining the function of a verb form or grammatical construction (§129). Further clarification is now required. In fact, in the account given so far the following criteria based on semantics and interpretation have emerged which play a part in the choice of verb forms or constructions in texts: simultaneous or prior action, single or repeated action, emphasis (mode of action, 'Aktionsart').

For example, these criteria show precisely why the chain of WAYYIQTOLs can be interrupted by WAW-x-QATAL: to express anteriority, simultaneity, contrast or emphasis (§§40-42, 48). Similarly, interruption by WAW-x-YIQTOL/weQATAL denotes a repeated action (§46). Also, the difference between the two constructions with a similar emphatic function—WAW-x-QATAL and WAW-x-YIQTOL— is that the first expresses a single action, the other a continuous or repeated action (§83); the same criterion explains why QATAL (-x) and weQATAL are used in the second member of the syntactic construction with protasis-apodosis (§113.1, 3).[87]

We need to add some qualifying remarks concerning the validity of the categories 'tense' and 'mode' of action. In Hebrew, Weinrich sees no validity in either as far as modern (and classical) languages are concerned.[88] Using text linguistics, he redefined the traditional teaching on 'tense(s)' in terms of linguistic perspective: degree zero comprises the present (in discourse = D), the imperfect and the simple past (in narrative = N); recovered information comprises the present perfect (in D) and the past perfect (in N); anticipated 'information' comprises the future (in D) and the conditional (in N). 'Mode', on the other hand, is seen by Weinrich in terms of prominence: the imperfect is the background tense, the (simple) past is the foreground tense. On this topic see §3.

As for Hebrew, I have already pointed out the need to avoid assigning a fixed tense equivalent for the various verbal forms, and establishing this equivalent from the tense used in modern translations. The first step is to find out the function of a particular tense (§132). Even so, I think that the various verbal forms and constructions should be distributed along the three fundamental 'temporal axes' (not 'tenses' strictly speaking), past, present, future. I think this solution is necessary because, unlike modern and classical languages, Hebrew does not have different forms for the simple past and the present perfect or for the imperfect and the simple past nor does it have different forms for background and foreground. In fact (cf. §135):

— the same YIQTOL form denotes the future in D and the conditional (= recovered information) in N and even repetition (= background) in N;
— the same QATAL form denotes the past (= recovered information) in N (= simple past or past perfect) and also in D (= present perfect);
— the simple nominal clause denotes the present (= degree zero) in D and also contemporaneity (= background) in both N and D;
— the compound nominal clause denotes background in N (= simple past, imperfect or past perfect) and even D (present perfect).

On the other hand, 'mode' of action (contemporaneity or anteriority, single or repeated action, emphasis) is important in the choice of verbal forms or constructions as indicated above.

I think, therefore, that only by combining the three criteria of temporal axes, mode (of action) and text linguistic level can the Hebrew verbal system be described in full (as I have attempted in §135). In contrast, the category of 'perfective-imperfective' or 'complete-incomplete' ('Aspekt') seems to me to be completely irrelevant.

(6) *The emphatic function and word-order in the clause*

§134. The emphatic function merits a separate study. Generally speaking, it coincides with first position in the clause not counting WAW.

Since there are no cases in Hebrew the word-order of clauses tends to be fixed.[89] In a verb clause the verb comes first and receives the emphasis of the sentence.[90] However, this normal word-order can be changed: a component other than the verb and on which the emphasis is required can be placed first (compound nominal clause).[91]

Now the component placed at the head of the clause can be nominal ('subject', 'object') or adverbial   (adverb, preposition + noun/infinitive). In such cases the function of the compound nominal clause is to indicate that the first component of the sentence is the predicate (x-QATAL, x-YIQTOL, §6).

§135.   It must be made clear that the criterion of emphasis cannot explain all the examples of change in order found in the texts.[92] This does not mean that the criterion of first position in the sentence is inadequate. As it happens, emphasis is only one of the functions dependent on word order and then only in the single clause. Once we go from the individual clause to more complex structures, the emphasis becomes too weak and the first position in the sentence takes on a different function. In general terms we can state that any change in the normal (word) order of the clause, which means every compound nominal clause (CNC) (§138), in both narrative and discourse, has the linguistic function of marking information as belonging not to the main thrust of communication (degree zero or foreground) but to the secondary level (antecedent or background).

In speaking of 'first position in the sentence' in the context of a syntactic structure longer than the single sentence, evidently the term 'sentence' has to be understood in a sense wide enough to include both the paragraph (protasis-apodosis) and narrative units of varying length, comprising antecedent and degree zero or degree zero and background. Now, the criterion of 'first position in the sentence' varies depending on which of these three settings it is in. In the single clause its function is to emphasize the first (non-verbal) element, which then becomes the predicate (CNC, §134). In the paragraph, instead, there is no emphasis on any individual term and the CNC indicates that the whole construction is not the main construction but circumstantial to the main clause (two-member syntactic construction). In the same way, in a narrative unit the CNC marks the action as an antecedent circumstance (antecedent) or a concomitant circumstance (background) to the principal action (degree zero or foreground). On this problem see §126.

Now, using the criterion of first position in the sentence together with the criterion of the three text-linguistic levels (linguistic attitude, prominence, linguistic perspective) all the verbal forms and grammatical constructions in Hebrew can be divided into two contrasting groups. See the following table.

N.B. In the table and the explanation which follows I use the following symbols:

↑	= recovered information	0	= degree zero
↓	= anticipated information	D	= discourse
Pr	= prominence	N	= narrative
LP	= linguistic perspective	CNC	= complex nominal clause
SNC	= simple nominal clause	fg	= foreground
VC	= verbal clause	bg	= background

Table 2

	Group I	LA	Pr	LP
1	narrative WAYYIQTOL	N	fg	0
2	direct volitive forms: —'EQTelA —imperative —(x-) jussive YIQTOL	D	fg	0
3	(x-) QATAL	D	fg	0
4	indirect volitive forms: —we'EQTeLA —uQeTOL —weYIQTOL	D	fg/bg	0/↓
5	x-indicative YIQTOL	D	fg	0
6	**Group II** כי אשל etc. + QATAL	N/D	bg	↑
7	(WAW-)x-QATAL	N/D	bg	↑
8	weQATAL	N D	bg fg	↓
9	(WAW-)x-YIQTOL	N D	bg fg	↓
10	SNC	N D	bg fg/bg	

	Group II	LA	Pr	LP
11	constructions of the apodosis: —WAYYIQTOL —QATAL —WAW-x-QATAL	N/D	fg	0
12	—weQATAL —YIQTOL —WAW-x-YIQTOL	N D D	bg fg fg	
13	—WAW-SNC	N D	bg fg	
14	constructions of the protasis: —x-QATAL —x-YIQTOL —SNC —conjunction + QATAL —conjunction + YIQTOL —weQATAL	N/D	bg	

Classification of verb forms and grammatical constructions
by position in the sentence and linguistic level

Group I (nos. 1-5 of Table 2)
This includes the forms and constructions which occur exclusively in N or exclusively in D. The choice depends on the LP. Some explanatory notes are needed, though.

Nos. 1-2. The verb is in first position and they each comprise an independent VC (§95, type 1). In respect of the LA they are different and so are exclusively N (WAYYIQTOL) or D (direct volitional forms). They are identical in respect of Pr (all fg) and of LP (all O) because they are independent VC. The x-jussive YIQTOL construction comprises a VC (not CNC) because it is the syntactic equivalent of initial jussive YIQTOL (§55.2).

No. 3. This is the report form (§§22-23) which also opens narrative discourse (§76). Even in this form x-QATAL comprises a VC (not a CNC) because it corresponds to simple QATAL. It heads the sentence and is found only in D so differing syntactically from retrospective QATAL (no. 6). Pr marks the fg and LP the O.

No. 4. They are all VC and occur only in D; accordingly I have put them in group I. Even so, they comprise an independent clause only when co-ordinated with an initial volitional form (usually in the same person, §64) (§95, type 1a). When, instead, they are dependent on a preceding jussive form (usually in a different person, §64), they comprise, syntactically, a dependent clause (§95, type 2) since they are not initial forms but continuation forms. They mark the fg or O, of the bg and ↓, depending on whether they are coordinate or subordinate. See the examples given in §§55, 61, 63, 65. It would be preferable if we could be more precise about the syntactic criteria for determining when they are coordinate and when subordinate.

No. 5. The most complex structure in group I. It is a fact that indicative YIQTOL is never in first position in a sentence (§55.1). Scholars have not noticed this, perhaps because they consider it to be irrelevant;[90] in the light of the present discussion, though, quite the opposite is true. As far as I can ascertain the only possible way of expressing the simple future (indicative) at the beginning of a discourse in Hebrew is to use precisely the x-YIQTOL construction. Whereas simple YIQTOL in first position would be a jussive the weQATAL can only open a speech but not continue one (§57). Does this mean that for the ancient Hebrews the simple future was always a result of something prior, a 'second position in the sentence'? It could do. It would certainly explain why a CNC is used to express the future.

Note that in D all three axes of time (present, past and future, or in text-linguistic terms: O, ↑, ↓ of LP, cf. §133) can be in the fg of the Pr (see the examples in §§52-53). In other words, all three axes of time (or the three levels of LP) can comprise a main line of communication (§92). This provides D with a very much greater variety of possibilities than is true of N where the fundamental axis (the past) is unavoidably fixed. It is another reason why there are fewer tense shifts in D than there are in N (cf. §94).

Group II (nos. 6-13 in Table 2)
It comprises verb forms and grammatical constructions occurring in both N and D; the LA is of no importance.

Nos. 6-7 (WAW-)-x-QATAL is one of the chief constructions in Group II. It comprises a CNC and so does not mark O of the LP but ↑, in both N and D. For D, however, see §167. For the same reason (WAW-)x-QATAL is in the main line not of communication but of the bg (§§86-87) when it follows the main verb; but when it precedes the main verb it is an antecedent construction (§88) or a protasis (§111). For discussion of these functions see §126.3-5.

In terms of the three text-linguistic levels (LA, Pr and LP), retrospective QATAL (preceded by אשר, כי etc. both in N, §8 and in D, §25) behaves very much like the (WAW-)x-QATAL, the difference being that it is a VC. The explanation for the similarity is that retrospective QATAL is never in initial position but always comes second in the sentence. This is also how QATAL in N is clearly distinct from the narrative WAYYIQTOL in spite of what is written in the grammars (§§14, 17).

Nos. 8-9. These are two more constructions which correspond in respect of the three linguistic levels; the difference is that (WAW-)x-YIQTOL is a CNC, weQATAL is a VC. Note, too, that weQATAL is an initial form in the single sentence but not in a narrative unit or in the narrative to which it belongs (§57). For this reason it behaves, syntactically, like the (WAW-)x-YIQTOL. See the remarks on the two previous constructions (nos. 6-7). In both the weQATAL and the (WAW-)x-YIQTOL there is a definite difference at the level of Pr. In D, in fact, the two constructions indicate fg of ↓ in the communication (= future) whereas in N they indicate the bg (= repetition) (§§156, 157, 163). There is a difference of this type not only in the axis of the future but also in the axis of the present (see no. 10) though not in that of the past (cf. nos. 6-7). See also under nos. 11-13. At the level of individual sentences the difference between weQATAL and (WAW-)x-YIQTOL is that as a CNC this second construction places the emphasis on the element 'x' both in D (§59) and in N (§46).

No. 10. It is typical of the SNC (and of the CNC) to occur both in N and in D but with one important difference. In D the SNC marks the fg of the communication (= present, §53) but it can also mark the bg (usually preceded by WAW, §§51, 54). In N, instead, it always indicates the bg (= contemporaneity, §43).

Nos. 11-13. Discussion of the constructions used in the apodosis can be found in §§126-127. Here it is worth noting that all the forms and constructions available in Hebrew, including the imperative (cf. Table 1) can occur in the apodosis. Accordingly we find the VC (WAYYIQTOL, QATAL, weQATAL, YIQTOL), the CNC (WAW-x-QATAL, WAW-x-YIQTOL) and the SNC. I have classed all these constructions in group II because they are found in both N and D. I have been unable to find examples of WAW-x-YIQTOL in N. Now, the presence of WAYYIQTOL in this list (also in D!) can only occasion surprise. In view of what has been said earlier (§126.2) the constructions of the apodosis are syntactically not initial but take second position in the paragraph. The result is that although they comprise the main clause they are not independent, either in terms of syntax (§95, type 2) or of meaning. If this analysis is allowed it would explain the presence of WAYYIQTOL in a D apodosis. It is not a narrative WAYYIQTOL which always has first position and is exclusive to narrative (no. 1). As regards syntactic state it is more like the continuation WAYYIQTOL (§146). Indeed, both have in common two basic characteristics: taking only second position in a unit of text, never the first and not having a tense of its own. Unlike the normal continuation WAYYIQTOL, though, the apodosis WAYYIQTOL denotes the fg and O of communication (see below).

From the aspect of Pr the various constructions of the apodosis comprise three sub-groups corresponding to the three basic axes: past (no. 11), future (no. 12) and present (no. 13). As has already been seen for these same constructions outwith the apodosis (see above, nos. 8-9), in the axes of the future and the present (but not the past) there is an analogous distinction.

On one side weQATAL, YIQTOL and WAW-x-YIQTOL in D denote the fg of the communication (=future) whereas in N they denote the bg (= repetition). On the other side, WAW-SNC denotes the fg (= present) in D but the bg (= contemporaneity) in N. For this cf. §113.

Consequently, in constructions of the apodosis the distinction connected with Pr (fg—bg) is retained but the distinction connected with LA (N—D) vanishes as does the distinction connected with LP (in practice they are all O).

No. 14. According to the list of §§107-108, 110, the constructions of the protasis comprising a complete sentence are: conjunction + finite verb (with QATAL = no. 6, or with YIQTOL), x-QATAL (= no. 7), x-YIQTOL (= no. 9) and SNC (= no. 10). On the basis of §120 two additional observations can be made. First, x-QATAL and x-YIQTOL (both CNC) are equivalent to clearly nominal constructions ('casus pendens', relative clause, participle, SNC). This confirms the non-verbal character of the CNC (§6). Second, the construction comprising conjunction + finite verbal form (QATAL or YIQTOL) is equivalent to an adverb or adverbial expression (preposition + noun or infinitive). Even weQATAL belongs to the category of adverb because when it occurs in the protasis it is equivalent to the construction conjunction + YIQTOL. The conclusion from these two remarks has to be that when a finite verbal form occurs in the protasis it takes second position in the sentence and can occur then only on that condition.[94] Otherwise, it is a second position construction as in the case of weQATAL (no. 8, above). All the constructions of the protasis with a finite verb form, therefore, belong to Group II. They have two characteristics: they are both grammatically and syntactically dependent (§95, type 3) and they can occur in both N and D. They are, then, indifferent with respect to AL. As for Pr, they denote the bg as they are all equivalent to a circumstance placed at the beginning of a sentence, like the 'casus pendens' (§120).

We can conclude that the two criteria for classifying all Hebrew verb forms and constructions (Table 2), namely, position in the sentence and the three linguistic levels combine and coincide to single out two distinctive and opposed sets. We can state that verb forms with first position in the sentence are also connected at all three linguistic levels, particularly at LA; they are thus exclusively N or exclusively D (Group I). In contrast, verb forms and constructions which are indifferent in respect of LA, i.e., which can occur in N or D, come second in the sentence or paragraph (Group II).

This conclusion shows yet again how the various criteria used in analysis (based on grammar, syntax or semantics) combine and validate each other (cf. §126). The same conclusion also proves the two basic principles adopted in the present study to be valid: the distinction between VC and CNC (§6) and the not unrelated syntactic importance of first position in the sentence. These two points comprise a definite stand concerning two very controversial problems. Let me say again that only analysis using some form of text linguistics can provide a consistent solution.

§136. The distinction established above (§126.3) between the complex nominal clause (x-QATAL) and the two-member syntactic construction (x = protasis/apodosis) can explain those cases where the meaning, in spite of using what appear to be identical constructions, suggests that in some the emphasis is on the dating formula which heads the clause but in others there is no emphasis at all. Constructions of the first type can be explained as compound noun clauses and those of the second as belonging to the syntactic construction with protasis and apodosis. Compare, for example, 1 Kgs 6.37 which uses the protasis-apodosis pattern:

1 Kgs 6.37

בשנה הרביעית יסר בית יהוה (38§)

1 Kgs 15.1

ובשנת . . . מלך אבים (37§)

This analysis of 1 Kgs 15.1 is confirmed by the parallel in 2 Chron. 13.1 which is clearly a two-member syntactic construction:

2 Chron. 13.1

בשנת . . . וימלך אביה (37§)

§137. For some of the constructions which can come first in the clause it is useful to analyse the list of different types drawn up by Bendavid (II, 800-801). The list on p. 800 contains mainly examples of the complex noun clause. Instead, the first list on p. 801 (described as 'emphasis before the end' of the sentence) chiefly comprises examples modelled on the two-member syntactic construction, with 'casus pendens' in the protasis and a compound noun clause in the apodosis. The second list on p. 801 (termed 'emphasis at the end' of the sentence) seems to be based on less certain criteria.

§138. A recent study by Muraoka re-examines the problem of word-order in Hebrew.[95] Basically, it confirms the traditional view that the normal order in the verb clause is V(erb)-S(ubject); however, it differs in many ways from the analysis proposed in these pages. Following K. Schlesinger's opinion Muraoka holds that the study of word-order requires examples with WAYYIQTOL to be left out as the word-order in such clauses is V-S of necessity; only examples without WAW consecutive can provide relevant data.[96]

I cannot see why it is precisely the WAYYIQTOL which should be left out of consideration since it is the normal type of narrative verbal clause.

There is no doubt, then, that the normal order of the narrative verb clause is V-S. Every variation of the kind S-V, apart from the WAW-x-QATAL construction just mentioned, must therefore be judged abnormal (since it comprises a compound nominal clause) and its function has to be determined (cf., for instance, the examples of interruption in the narrative chain, §§40ff.).

Analysis of the verb clause of discourse is definitely more complicated. Most cases of clauses without the 'WAW consecutive', where the word-order is S–V, belong to the category of discourse, as Muraoka himself accepts ('conversational texts').[97] Even in these cases, though, the S–V order shows that the clauses are not verbal but compound nominal clauses (cf. §6.1). Exceptions are the x-jussive YIQTOL construction (§135, no. 2) and the x-QATAL report construction (§135, no. 5). The inevitable conclusion is that in the verb clause of discourse, too, normal word-order is V–S.

Now, changes in the normal sequence, in compound nominal clauses both in narrative and in discourse, can be explained within the limits of the single sentence (emphasis) or within longer linguistic units; they follow syntactic models which are alike in both narrative and discourse.[95] For this see the foregoing discussions on the YIQTOL and x-YIQTOL forms in discourse (§55), on the two-member syntactic pattern in both narrative and discourse (§126) and on first position in the sentence (§135).

b. *Forms and constructions*

§139. We will go on to inspect each of the verb forms and grammatical constructions, listing their functions in the various contexts, applying the analysis set out above. A word of caution though: as this account of syntax is only a first draft the list of functions cannot be complete. Even so, I think that even if a wider range of texts were to be studied no major changes would be required.

(1) *WAYYIQTOL*

§140. In respect of linguistic attitude, WAYYIQTOL is the tense for narrative (§81); in respect of emphasis it denotes the foreground (§86); in respect of linguistic aspect it denotes degree zero (§88).

It chiefly denotes succession as can be determined indirectly from the principles of morphology and syntax, by establishing why the narrative chain is interrupted (§§40ff.)[96] It can instead mark a conclusion, even if more rarely, and this can sometimes be determined using criteria which do not derive from morphology but are literary and semantic (cf., for example, §38; similarly in 'narrative speech' also, §75).

§141.   In the antecedent, WAYYIQTOL can continue one of the constructions used for this function; in such cases its tense depends on the tense of the preceding construction: imperfect (cf. 2 Kgs. 12.10b-12, §35; Job 1.2-3, §90), pluperfect (cf. 1 Sam. 28.3, §27; Gen. 39.1, §91) and also the simple past.

§142.   In 'narrative comment' WAYYIQTOL also retains the tense of the preceding construction (§84). In this case the WAYYIQTOL can also express an action which the context clearly shows is repeated, as in:

Judges 6

3	והיה אם־זרע ישראל
	ועלה מדין ועמלק ובני־קדם
	ועלו עליו
4	<u>ויחנו עליהם</u>
	<u>וישחיתו את־יבול הארץ עד־בואך עזה</u>
	<u>ולא־ישאירו</u> מחיה בישראל ושה שור וחמור

3   Now when Israel had sown
    Madian, Amalek and the sons of the East came up;
    they came up against them,
4   they camped against them.
    they destroyed all the produce of the land as far as Gaza
    and left no means of subsistence, neither sheep nor bull nor
    ass.

The repetitive value of WAYYIQTOL (v. 4) depends on the preceding weQATALs (v. 3); note that in this case the corresponding negative of WAYYIQTOL is ולא + YIQTOL, but for a single, past action it is ולא + QATAL (§40).

§143.   In 'narrative discourse' WAYYIQTOL is never initial but continues the form (x-)QATAL of report, retaining the same linguistic perspective and the same tense; the negative form is ולא + QATAL as with the WAYYIQTOL of true narrative (§76). It can also continue a simple noun clause with or without a participle (§77).
    A WAYYIQTOL can also continue the construction with הנה (cf. 2 Sam. 19.2, §68). In this case it expresses an antecedent action and its tense depends on the discursive context in which it occurs (present perfect).

§144. Lastly, WAYYIQTOL occurs in the apodosis of the two-member syntactic construction in both narrative and discourse (§113.1).

§145. Since it is a macro-syntactic marker of narrative (§36) *wayehi* does not behave like an ordinary WAYYIQTOL as it does not comprise an independent clause nor alter in any way the syntactic structure of the sentence (§127).
For WAYYIQTOL in poetry see below (§§172-174).

§146. It is clear, then, that text linguistic analysis enables us to formulate a set of rules concerning the use of WAYYIQTOL and so considerably lessen the frustrating impression gained from leafing through traditional grammars: that almost any tense of modern languages can be used to translate it (§1). To complete the picture it must be emphasized that the various functions of WAYYIQTOL listed in the preceding paragraphs have not been invented to explain the different tenses this verb form takes on in the various contexts. In fact, everything is based on a syntactic distinction connected with the criterion of first position in the sentence (§§134-135). By the same criterion a distinction has to be made between two types of WAYYIQTOL which grammatically are identical but in terms of text syntax are different: (1) narrative WAYYIQTOL, (2) continuation WAYYIQTOL.
(1) WAYYIQTOL is a narrative form when it occurs at the beginning of an independent unit of text (cf. §36) and when it belongs to a chain of identical narrative forms (§140). It marks the foreground and zero degree of communication and has a corresponding fixed tense (simple past).
(2) WAYYIQTOL is a continuation form when it belongs to a text which begins with a non-WAYYIQTOL construction. The requirement for this definition is to be able to establish that such a WAYYIQTOL does not comprise the beginning of a narrative in the true sense. Normally this can be determined with no difficulty. But there can be a problem when a narrative unit opens with a complex antecedent (§91). Nevertheless, at the theoretical level at least, the difference between an initial or narrative WAYYIQTOL and a continuation WAYYIQTOL can be clearly set out as follows:

antecedent construction → continuation WAYYIQTOL complex antecedent ('short independent narrative', §27): e.g. Job 1.1-5 (§90): Gen. 39.1-6 (§91)	narrative WAYYIQTOL start of a true narrative (cf. §§16-19)

It is clear, therefore, that the essential difference is the following: a narrative WAYYIQTOL is in first position whereas a continuation WAYYIQTOL is in second position. For this reason the continuation WAYYIQTOL has no linguistic level or tense of its own but acquires the tense of the preceding construction.

We can now classify the initial constructions we have found to occur as antecedents of a continuation WAYYIQTOL:

(a) antecedent (§141), Job 1.1, 4; Gen. 39.1:

—(WAW-)x-QATAL
—weQATAL

(b) narrative comment (§142), 2 Kgs 17.34, 40b; Judg. 6.3:

—simple nominal clause
—weQATAL

(c) narrative discourse (§143), Judg. 11.15; Josh. 24.17; Exod. 6.2b:

                                    continuation
                                    WAYYIQTOL

—(x-)QATAL
—simple noun clause

(d) discourse (§143), 2 Sam. 19.2:

—הנה + simple noun clause

(e) Another way the continuation WAYYQITOL is used needs to be noted: to continue an explanatory or causal phrase expressed by אשר or כי + 'retrospective' QATAL, both in narrative (§8) and in discourse (§25). For example:

2 Kgs 17.7

ויהי
. . . כי־חטאו בני־ישראל ליהוה אלהיהם
ויראו אלהים אחרים
(. . . series of WAYYIQTOLs in coordination with the foregoing)

This happened
because the children of Israel had sinned against
Yahweh, their God...
and had revered other gods...

Gen. 3.17

כי שמעת לקול אשתך

ותאכל מן־העץ ...

Since you listened to the word ('voice') of your wife
and ate from the tree

(f) The WAYYIQTOL which occurs in the apodosis in both narrative
and discourse (§144) is like the continuation WAYYIQTOL. The
difference between the two is that the WAYYIQTOL of apodosis
indicates the degree zero of communication (§135, no. 11).

(g) *wayehi* (the macro-syntactic marker of narrative, §145) is also
similar to the continuation WAYYIQTOL as it is a second position
construction within the independent narrative unit (§36) and can
also occur in discourse (§78). The difference here is that the
continuation WAYYIQTOL has verbal force within the single
sentence but the force of *wayehi* is within the paragraph (§127.2).

There is, then, quite a variety of constructions which can act as
antecedent to a continuation WAYYIQTOL (types a-e). Their only
common characteristic is that the action takes place in the past, even
after הנה (present perfect because the action is portrayed in terms of
the present situation, §68). In the other types the action can be prior,
single, repeated, etc. depending on the tense of the initial construction.

One remaining problem, however, must be mentioned which has
yet to be examined in depth: what is the factor which determines the
choice of the continuation WAYYIQTOL? The problem is evident
from a comparison vv. 1-2 of Job 1 with vv. 4-5 (§90).

vv. 1-2	vv. 4-5
איש היה ...	והלכו בניו
והיה האיש ההוא ...	ועשו משתה ...
	ושלחו
	וקראו ...
ויולדו לו ...	ויהי ...

The problem can be set out in these terms: why is there a
continuation WAYYIQTOL immediately after the weQATAL in
vv. 1-2 when in vv. 4-5 the weQATAL is continued by three more

weQATALs and only then by a continuation WAYYIQTOL? The continuation WAYYIQTOL and the weQATAL appear to be completely interchangeable here. Is there a criterion for the choice of one over the other? As yet I can provide no answer to this question.

(2) QATAL

§147.   QATAL is neutral in respect of linguistic attitude and occurs in both narrative and speech. Its function is principally 'retrospective' in narrative (§§8, 81) and in speech (§25); in neither, therefore, does it express the foreground (of prominence: §§86-87) or the degree zero of linguistic aspect (§§88, 92). The conclusion is that QATAL is not a narrative form as has already been noted several times (cf. §§14-15, for example).

§148.   In the apodosis of the two-member syntactic construction QATAL expresses the degree zero of narrative in quite an exceptional way (§126.1); the same applies to the apodosis of constructions expressing time, with or without *wayehi* (§127.1). Remember that it is not always possible to differentiate clearly between this construction and the outwardly similar complex nominal clause where QATAL is not purely narrational but 'emphatic' (§§126.3, 136).

§149.   Noteworthy in discourse is the QATAL of the 'report', either clause-initial or preceded by a subject (x-QATAL (§§22-23). The marked contrast which is evident when the same event is first narrated by a WAYYIQTOL, then reported in direct speech using QATAL is the syntactic setting which best explains the nature of the two forms in terms of the linguistic categories of narrative (WAYYIQTOL) and comment (QATAL).
This type of QATAL develops into 'narrative discourse' (§76).

§150.   When preceded by a preposition (עקב, כי etc.), QATAL occurs in the protasis of the two-member syntactic construction, both in narrative and in speech (§101).

§151.   For the meaning of QATAL in speech when preceded by *hinneh* see §67. For the 'performative' QATAL see note 46.

§152. The non-narrative use of QATAL indicated by text linguistic analysis goes against the common opinion of grammarians. This has led Schneider to a forceful conclusion, though it is only expressed in a footnote: 'In reality, then, the perfect is not a tense as it is neutral in respect of the basic opposition: narrative/commentary'.[100] On the other hand, Gross has shown Schneider to be wrong by a *reductio ad absurdum*: 'Since succession in the past is also expressed by WAYYIQTOL in speech (. . .) to be consistent Schneider would have had to claim the same about WAYYIQTOL as well and so attain absurdity'.[101]

I think that Gross is only partly correct. It is true that WAYYIQTOL is also used in speech but that is no reason for claiming this to be its normal use (§146). On the contrary, as it is the non-narrative use of QATAL which is normal, his argument of *reductio ad absurdum*, in my opinion, is not convincing. My own view is that Schneider's conclusion is basically correct; indeed, it should have been stated clearly in the body of the text. Even so, the special case of the apodosis in the two-member construction (and in the constructions expressing time with or without a preceding *wayehi*) needs to be noted. There the QATAL is a form of degree zero even though it is in second position (as is always the case in narrative, §76). This can be explained from the syntax of the sentence with protasis and apodosis (§126.2).

(3) *YIQTOL*

§153. This is the tense for speech as against WAYYIQTOL, the tense for narrative (§§7, 51, 81). With the criterion of position within the sentence two types of YIQTOL can be identified: one a jussive which normally is in first position, the other an indicative which is never in first position (§§55, 64). See also §135 (nos. 2 and 5).

As for prominence, YIQTOL and the volitional forms (§87) denote the foreground; with regard to linguistic aspect, the jussive YIQTOL expresses degree zero and the indicative, anticipated information (§92).

In rare cases the indicative form does not express the simple future as it normally does, but a repeated or continued action in the past, in much the same way as in narrative. See 2 Sam. 15.34 (§103) and Exod. 3.14 (cf. the article cited in note 83). Another clear example is:

Jer. 36.18

Baruch replied:

מפיו יקרא אלי את־כל־הדברים האלה
ואני כתב על־הספר בדיו

'From his (Jeremiah's) mouth did he utter to me all these
words,
while I wrote on the book in ink'.

§154.   In narrative, too, YIQTOL expresses anticipated information
(linguistic perspective: §88).

§155.   Preceded by a conjunction (אשר, כי, אם) YIQTOL is used in
the protasis of the two-member syntactic construction in discourse as
well as in narrative (§§97-99; cf. §135, no. 14).
    Occasionally it also occurs in the apodosis of the same syntactic
construction to denote the future (in discourse) or a repeated action
(in narrative) (§§113.3, 118, 135, no. 12). The same applies when the
protasis is preceded by *wayehi* (§34).

(4) *weQATAL*[102]

§156.   The form weQATAL, usually termed 'inverted perfect',
occurs in speech as well as in narrative to denote the future and
repetition respectively. It comes first in the individual sentence but
can never begin an independent unit of narrative or discourse (§57).
That is, it is always preceded by a different construction either of
discourse or of narrative which it continues. The form והיה enjoys
greater independence than a normal weQATAL which might lead to
it being considered initial. In fact this is not the case. The greater
autonomy of והיה is explained by its syntactic status which has an
analogy in that of *wayehi* (§127.2). Like *wayehi* the function of והיה is
not in the individual sentence but in the unit of discourse or
narrative to which it belongs. This function consists in placing the
circumstance, or rather the paragraph which follows it (= two-
member syntactic pattern, for example Exod. 33.8-9) within the main
thrust of the message and of connecting this with the preceding
context.
    In speech, when continuing a volitional form, weQATAL simply
qualifies the action as future (with a nuance of succession or
conclusion) unlike the weYIQTOL (§§61-65, 159).

It occurs at times in a chain of weQATALs to indicate a series of orders/instructions; its equivalent is the WAYYIQTOL chain expressing the execution of the same orders/instructions when an individual action is involved (§§57-59). The same form weQATAL is kept, though, even in the fulfilment when the action expressed is continuous or repeated (§60).

As for linguistic levels, weQATAL in discourse denotes the foreground or anticipated information, according to the type of the preceding construction; in narrative, however, it denotes background (§135, no. 8).

§157.   In narrative, weQATAL denotes a repeated action; this is how it can be differentiated from simple QATAL expressing a single action. It also expresses repeated action in the antecedent (§90); within a narrative it can also break a chain of WAYYIQTOLs, where it can be replaced by the equivalent WAW-x-YIQTOL construction (§82).

§158 (i)   The weQATAL preserves the same functions of expressing the future (in speech) and repeated action (in narrative) in the apodosis of the two-member syntactic construction (§113.1) and also when *wayehi* precedes the protasis (§35). When weQATAL occurs in the protasis, either in narrative or in discourse (§97) it is the syntactical equivalent of the conjunction + YIQTOL construction (§135, no. 14).

§158 (ii)   Some special cases must be noted where a type of weQATAL occurs which is not the 'inverted form' discussed up till now denoting the future or repetition. Instead it expresses a single past action.

(1) In most of the examples known to me this weQATAL is a continuation form of a narrative WAYYIQTOL, apparently with the same tense, as comparison between Exod. 8.11 and 9.34 shows:

Exod. 8.11 (EVV 15)

וירא פרעה כי היתה הרוחה
... והכבד את־לבו
Pharaoh saw that there had been a respite (of the plague) and he hardened his heart...

Exod. 9.34

וירא פרעה כי־חדל המטר והברד והקלת
ויסף לחטא
<u>ויכבד</u> לבו הוא ועבדיו

Pharaoh saw that the rain and the hail and the thunderclaps had ceased
and he continued to sin
and hardened his heart, he and his servants.

Likewise in 2 Kgs 18.36:

2 Kgs 18.28b

וידבר ויאמר
(direct speech up to v. 35)

18.36

<u>והחרישו</u> העם . . .

28b Then (Sennacherib's envoy) spoke and said. . .
36 And the people remained silent.

The parallel Isa. 36.21 has instead:

. . . <u>ויחרישו</u>

Other examples of this type are:

Judg. 3.23

ויצא . . .
ויסגר . . .
<u>ונעל</u> . . .

(Ehud) went out. . .
(he) shut. . .
and locked. . .

1 Sam. 17.38

 וילבש . . .
<u>ונתן</u> . . .
<u>וילבש</u> . . .

(Saul) made (David) wear (his armour)
and placed (a bronze helmet on his head)
and made him wear (a coat of mail).

1 Kgs 14.27

‫ויעש ...‬
‫והפקיד ...‬

= 2 Chron. 12.10

(Rehoboam) made (bronze shields)
and entrusted them...

Another text to be noted, which is quite long, is 2 Kgs 23.4-15, where a series of WAYYIQTOLs is continued by weQATAL.[103]

In terms of what we know about Hebrew syntax it has to be said that these examples of a continuation weQATAL denoting the past are exceptional. The tense shift WAYYIQTOL → weQATAL does occur, it is true, but it marks a distinct interruption of the narrative flow, with a transition from narrative to comment, and the weQATAL denotes a repeated action (§46).[104]

(2) In other examples weQATAL is a continuation of the emphatic construction x-QATAL (cf. §6.2):

2 Kgs 18.4 (§48)

‫הוא הסיר ...‬
‫ושבר ...‬
‫וכרת ...‬
‫וכתת ...‬

He (Hezekiah) it was who removed (the high places)
and smashed (the stelas)
and cut down (the Asherah)
and broke in pieces (the bronze serpent).

1 Kgs 6

33	‫וכן עשה ...‬
	(list of deeds up to v. 34)
35	‫וקלע ...‬
	‫וצפה ...‬
33	And so he (Solomon) did...
35	and carved (the cherubim)...
	and overlaid them (with gold).

This usage of weQATAL for the past also appears to be exceptional.

(3) Finally, weQATAL comprises the apodosis of the two-member syntactic construction:

1 Kgs 6.32

ושתי דלתות עצי־שמן

וקלע עליהם . . .

וצפה . . .

וירד . . .

As for the two doors of olivewood (cf. v. 31)
he carved (on them. . .)
and overlaid them (with gold)
and hammered (gold on the cherubim. . .).

This tense of weQATAL is exceptional as well. In the apodosis of the two-member syntactic construction, in fact, weQATAL expresses the future (in discourse) or a continued action (in narrative) while the past is expressed by the simple QATAL or WAYYIQTOL (cf. §§113.1, 3; 114). The 'correct' construction occurs in the verses which come immediately before the passage quoted, if—as it seems—the nominal element preceding the verb is a 'casus pendens' (cf. §§124-125):

1 Kgs 6

29	ואת כל־קירות הבית מסב
	קלע . . .
30	ואת־קרקע הבית
	צפה . . .
31	ואת פתח הדביר
	עשה . . .

29   All the walls of the temple round about
       he carved. . .
30   The floor of the temple
       he overlaid. . .
31   The entrance to the debir
       he made. . .

Also noteworthy is 2 Kgs 11.1 where the ketib has: 'casus pendens' in the protasis and וְרָאֲתָה in the apodosis whereas the qere suggests the expected reading רָאֲתָה. In fact it occurs in the parallel 2 Chron. 22.10 (§104).

In all the three cases referred to above we might be tempted to correct the text and this is just what scholars do. However, in my opinion it would be prudent to collect other examples and classify them in order to obtain a wider picture before forming a definitive conclusion.

(5) *weYIQTOL*[102]

§159.   This is a non-initial construction used in speech. Its function is to continue a direct volitional form in order to express another volitional action ('indirect jussive'), usually to denote purpose; this is how it differs from weQATAL (§156) with which it usually co-occurs (§§55, 61-64). The weYIQTOL is used to convey a general command. Should it be necessary to clarify a detail of the same order the 'emphatic' WAW-x-YIQTOL construction is used (§57). Besides this subordinating function (syntactic hypotaxis, §95, type 2) weYIQTOL is also used to coordinate a preceding jussive form (usually in the same person, §64) (parataxis, §95, type 1a). In each case only the context can determine which of these two functions is present (cf. §135, no. 4).

§160.   Accordingly, weYIQTOL expresses a volitive rather than a simple future. This is why it does not occur in the apodosis (§113). However, I am aware of two surprising cases: Josh. 3.13 and 2 Chron. 24.11 (§35). In the first example we find ויעמדו continuing a preceding x-YIQTOL construction (apodosis in a speech; the protasis is introduced by והיה). In the second example three weYIQTOLs occur (וישאהו, וישיבהו, ויערו) which continue a weQATAL (apodosis in a narrative; the protasis is introduced by *wayehi*). Other examples need to be found, though, before a final conclusion can be reached.

(6) *Simple noun clause (SNC)*

§161.   Though important in both discourse and narrative it is used differently in each category.

In discourse the SNC has a twofold function, expressing foreground (prominence: §86) or degree zero (linguistic perspective: §92) as well as background (prominence again: §87). It is often preceded by הנה (§68).

§162.   In narrative the function of the SNC, often preceded by WAW, is to provide comment by describing an action simultaneous with the main action. In this function it breaks the narrative chain of WAYYIQTOLs (§43) to denote the background for the action (prominence: §86). When the shift WAYYIQTOL → SNC is repeated in a text and the SNC becomes particularly long we have a 'commenting narrative' (§83). The SNC also occurs in the 'narrative comment' where it becomes narrative (§84).

Further, it is one of the constructions expressing an antecedent in order to denote simultaneous action (§§18, 19, 91).

In the two-member syntactic construction it occurs in the protasis to denote simultaneity in both narrative and speech (§100) and in the apodosis to denote the present (in speech) or simultaneity (in narrative: §113.2). See §135, nos. 10 and 14.

Finally, the simple noun clause with or without the participle can begin a 'narrative discourse' (§77).

(7) *The compound nominal clause (CNC)*

§163.   This includes the (WAW-)x-QATAL and (WAW-)x-YIQTOL constructions, in which the conjunction WAW is always optional, with no effect on their function.

In narrative the constructions are used in similar ways. In the antecedent, WAW-x-QATAL expresses a single action (often translated by the pluperfect) whereas WAW-x-YIQTOL expresses a repeated action (§§16, 18, 19, 91).

Further, WAW-x-QATAL interrupts the WAYIQTOL chain to denote a prior circumstance, simultaneity, contrast or prominence (background, §§40-42, 48); in the same situation WAW-x-YIQTOL denotes a repeated action and can be replaced by weQATAL (§46). Note that in such cases the determining factor for choosing between a construction with QATAL or one with YIQTOL is the type of action to be denoted, single or repeated respectively (§133).

§164.   In the two-member syntactic construction x-QATAL is used in the protasis (§105) and WAW-x-QATAL in the apodosis (also in speech: §113.1). In this formulation the WAW-x-QATAL construction denotes foreground (prominence: §86) and degree zero of the narrative (linguistic perspective: §88) only in exceptional cases (§126.1); the same applies to constructions expressing time with or without a preceding *wayehi* (§127.3).

§165.   In discourse x-YIQTOL and x-QATAL are foreground constructions with the function of emphasising the element 'x' (= predicate, §6.3). Also, the background construction WAW-x-YIQTOL interrupts the chain of weQATALs and has the corresponding function of emphasising the element 'x' (§§57-60, 85). The equivalent construction in narrative is WAW-x-QATAL with respect to the WAYYIQTOL chain (§163).

§166. The only function of WAW-x-QATAL in discourse apparently is to express a circumstance prior to the principal action or the background (§§54, 87).

§167. The CNC can function syntactically at the level of the single sentence or at the level of a paragraph or a narrative- or discourse-unit. At the level of the single sentence it shows that the predicate is not the finite verb but the nominal or adverbial element which comes first in the (WAW-)x-QATAL and (WAW-)x-YIQTOL constructions. In this way it is clearly distinct from the verbal sentence (§6). Note, however, that the x-QATAL construction for reporting comprises a verbal clause (not a CNC) because it can replace the initial QATAL (§135, no. 3) and therefore places no emphasis on the first element in the sentence. The x-indicative YIQTOL construction has no emphasis either (except in special cases, §56) but its syntactic status is still unclear (§135, no. 5). In both narrative and discourse the CNC sometimes indicates an emphasis on the non-verb component of a clause even when it is a background construction (§165). In such cases the CNC still remains a background form but has a degree of autonomy not shared by its foreground form.

At the level of the paragraph, or the unit of narrative or discourse the CNC indicates that the sentence does not come under the main thrust of communication but is syntactically dependent on the form of degree zero, even though grammatically it comprises a main clause. As a result it loses its emphatic function at the level of the single sentence gaining a wider syntactic function (§126.4). This happens when the CNC occurs in the protasis or the apodosis (§164), when it comprises the antecedent and when it is a background construction (§163). Note, however, that the CNC sometimes has emphatic function even when it is a background construction (see above).

Consequently, in the narrative unit the CNC does not indicate the foreground (prominence) or degree zero (linguistic perspective); instead it is basically a commenting or background construction. The exceptional use of a CNC as a foreground or zero degree construction in the apodosis (§164) is due to the special syntactic character of the two-member construction (cf. §126.2).

Table 3: First position in the sentence (§§95, 135)

Verb in 1st position	Verb in 2nd position

= VC
=independent clause
 	
N = narrative WAYYIQTOL
	= CNC
	= chiefly dependent clause
	   (§167)
	N/D: CNC denoting
	   —antecedent (WAW-x-QATAL,
	      WAW-x-YIQTOL)
	   —background (WAW-x-QATAL,
	      WAW-x-YIQTOL)
	   —protasis (x-QATAL, x-YIQTOL)
	   —apodosis (WAW-x-QATAL,
	      WAW-x-YIQTOL)
	   —simple future (?) (x-YIQTOL)

2nd position VC in the paragraph in the narrative unit or the unit of discourse	

	N/D: continuation-WAYYIQTOL
	(§ 146)
	   wayehi (§ 127.2)
	   WAYYIQTOL of apodosis
	   weQATAL (including והיה)
	   QATAL ⎫
	   YIQTOL ⎬of apodosis
	   weQATAL⎭
	   conjunction + QATAL/
	   YIQTOL

N.B. D = discourse, N = narrative, CNC = compound noun clause, VC = verb clause	

Table 4: Basic structures of Hebrew prose (§ 126)

(A) *circumstance*	→	main clause
(1) *protasis*	→	apodosis (=2SC)
(2) antecedent	→	narrative WAYYIQTOL (= narrative unit)

(A1) Second position constructions in the sentence comprise both those of the protasis (§95, type 3) and those of the apodosis (§95, type 2). The connection between protasis and apodosis is particularly close as neither can exist on its own even though the apodosis is the main clause (§ 135, nos. 11-13). The *wayehi* makes the 2SC 'verbal' and in consequence links it with the narrative thread of degree zero (§ 127.2).

(A2) The antecedent is a second position construction in the sentence whereas WAYYIQTOL is a first position verbal construction. The connection between antecedent and the narrative WAYYIQTOL, therefore, is not so close as the corresponding connection in the 2SC. Grammatically, the antecedent construction is independent; syntactically, it is dependent (§95, type 2).

(B) main clause	→	circumstance
(1) WAYYIQTOL at degree zero	→	אשר, כי, etc. + retrospective QATAL
(2) foreground WAYYIQTOL	→	background construction

(B1) Here with respect to the circumstance the connection is close because conjunction+QATAL is a second position construction which is also grammatically dependent (§95, type 3). In contrast, the WAYYIQTOL is a narrative form which is independent in every way.

(B2) Here the connection is not so close as in B1 because the background constructions belong to the second position; they are, therefore, syntactically dependent on the WAYYIQTOL but grammatically they comprise a main clause (§95, type 2).

N.B. 2SC = two-member syntactic construction

Chapter 10

COMMENTS ON THE USE OF TENSE IN POETRY

a. *Introductory remarks*

§168. Watson has written a good, up-to-date compendium on Hebrew poetry.[106]

On word-pairs, one of the basic components of poetry, mention must be made of Dahood,[107] who elucidated over 700 word-pairs common to Ugaritic and Hebrew, and of Avishur[108] who extended the field of research to other Semitic literature.[109]

Watters[110] has also contributed by using the topic of word-pairs and other repeated phrases ('formulae') as a 'criterion' of literary criticism to determine the unity or otherwise of lengthy verse compositions. The criterion is valid, but the conclusions drawn by Watters are based on too narrow a selection of 'formulae' to be acceptable in every instance.[111]

§169. Study of poetry has to be based on the MT, the traditional consonantal text as vocalized and therefore interpreted by the Masoretes several centuries later. Intense debate on the value of this Masoretic vocalization has been provoked in recent years, especially since the publication of Dahood's revolutionary translation of the Psalms[112] where the Masoretic vocalisation was deliberately ignored in order to determine the original meaning of the consonantal text using Northwest Semitic philology.[113]

In my opinion, although mistrust on principle is to be avoided, scholars should give preference to the consonantal text and feel free to change the vocalization when necessary. This is in any case quite a common practice among specialists. On the other hand the pruning away of conjunctions and other particles considered to be superfluous in poetry—a custom adopted chiefly by Cross, Freedman and their school—seems speculative.[114]

§170.   It is at least likely that for the use of verb forms poetry had its own rules which were not the same as for prose. This is why I consider it necessary to discuss the topic in a completely separate way (cf. §173).

The following account provides only a simple outline and the problem of how verb forms are used in poetry requires further research.[115]

b. *The problem*

§171.   Although it is possible to obtain a reasonably consistent account of how verb forms are used in prose, for poetry the problem is much more complicated and debated.

(1) The poetry of Ugarit has clearly shown that YIQTOL can be used as a form for past narrative; the same form is also used for the present and the future: in other words, it is universal as regards tense. This phenomenon also occurs in the archaic poetry of the Pentateuch (e.g. Gen. 49; Exod. 15; Num. 23-24; Judg. 5; Deut. 32-33) and in certain Psalms (e.g. 18; 29; 78) where YIQTOL even if not preceded by WAW, is generally used for any 'tense' including the past.

This archaic use of YIQTOL for the past has also been preserved in biblical prose, in certain fixed constructions, for example אז + YIQTOL (but אז + QATAL also occurs) and טרם + YIQTOL (but it also occurs with QATAL). Some scholars think that the WAYYIQTOL form should also be explained as a survival of YIQTOL=past preceded by WAW (like אז and טרם); accordingly, the expressions 'WAW conversive/inverse' should be replaced by 'conservative WAW'.[116]

§172.   (2) Characteristic of Canaanite and biblical poetry is the use of the forms YIQTOL and QATAL for the same tense in parallel lines. Previously this was considered suspect and often corrected by scholars; but the poetry of Ugarit has shown it to be perfectly legitimate.

Cassuto[117] drew attention to several examples of the pairing of the verb forms YIQTOL/QATAL or QATAL/YIQTOL from the same verbal root:

Hos. 5.5

> וישראל ואפרים יכשלו בעונם
> כשל גם יהודה עמם

Israel and Ephraim stumbled in their iniquity,
Judah, too, shall stumble with them.

Ps. 38.12

> אהבי ורעי מנגד נגעי יעמדו
> וקרובי מרחק עמדו

My friends and my companions stand afar off from my plague
and my kinsmen stand at a distance.

Ps. 93.3

> נשאו נהרות יהוה
> נשאו נהרות קולם
> ישאו נהרות דכים

May the rivers raise, O Yahweh,
may the rivers raise their voice,
may the rivers raise their floods.

Even when prefixed with a WAW the tense of YIQTOL does not change:

Isa. 60.16

> וינקת חלב גוים
> ושד מלכים תינקי

You shall suck the milk of the peoples
and the breast of kings shall you suck.

Amos 7.4

> ותאכל את־תהום רבה
> ואכלה את־החלק

And it (the fire) consumed the vast ocean
and it consumed the earth.

Ps. 29.10

> יהוה למבול ישב
> וישב יהוה מלך לעולם

Yahweh sits (enthroned) on the flood,
as a king Yahweh sits for ever.

Held[118] has added another example to those collected by Cassuto:

Prov. 11.7

במות אדם רשע תאבד תקוה
ותוחלת אונים אברה

At the death of the evil man hope perishes,
and the expectancy of the rich man[119] perishes.

In addition, Gevirtz[120] has shown that this characteristic alternation of YIQTOL/QATAL also occurs in the Amarna Letters written by the city rulers of Palestine, Phoenicia and Syria in Akkadian (the diplomatic language of that period, the 14th century BCE) influenced by peculiarities of the local language which was Canaanite.

Finally, it can be noted that the alternation YIQTOL//QATAL or QATAL//YIQTOL is of course also attested between verbs of different roots.[121]

§173.   (3) This phenomenon (§172) indicates that verb forms in poetry do not have a fixed tense. This is why it is advisable not to examine the verb systems of biblical poetry and prose together, as in the standard grammars, but quite separately, as we have already stated.

Recently, some authors who do not agree that poetry and prose follow different sets of rules have looked for a single system to explain both. One such is Gross[122] who rejects the common opinion that in poetry, especially late poetry, all the verb forms can be used to express the present. Instead, he argues that WAYYIQTOL (like QATAL) denotes the perfected, completed aspect of an action, in direct contrast with the lengthened form of YIQTOL. WAYYIQTOL, then would not be a true past tense but would express more the aspect (completed) of an action without having a tense of its own. However, even Gross has to admit some difficulty in analysing certain texts such as Psalm 29 and Job.[123] Besides, in my opinion the problem of verb forms cannot be resolved by appealing to the aspect of an action (§133); there have been many such attempts but it seems to me that the examples upset any fixed pattern. An approach which would yield useful results has been suggested above (note 94).

§174.   (4) What was the guiding criterion in poetry for choosing between the various verb forms? This problem has yet to receive a complete answer. Style, the desire for variety, the chiastic arrangement of constituents (for example, WAYYIQTOL [+ subject] //

WAW-subject-QATAL, a sequence also found in prose, cf. §86), etc. can explain some of the cases; but well-defined criteria which can throw light on the problem as a whole have yet to be found. Whereas prose usually provides clear indications of the tense when the action takes place (e.g. הנה, והיה, ויהי, particles, adverbs) poetry often gives no such clues. The tense of a verb form, therefore, has to be determined on the basis of context and other exegetical factors. This explains the differences, often quite marked, among the various translations.

NOTES

1. L. McFall, *The Enigma of the Hebrew Verbal System*, Sheffield, 1982.

2. H.-P. Müller, 'Zur Geschichte des hebräischen Verbs—Diachronie der Konjugationsthemen', *BZ* 27 (1983) 34-57; 'Ebla und das althebräische Verbalsystem', *Bib* 65 (1984), 145-67.

3. H. Weinrich, *Tempus. Besprochene und erzählte Welt*, 3rd edn, Stuttgart, 1977. Page references are to the 4th edn, 1985.

4. Weinrich, 5.

5. For a more detailed explanation see §§81ff., below.

6. Cf. Schneider, 207, addition to §48, 4.3; Talstra II, 34.

7. Weinrich, 171-72.

8. The first edition of the grammar came out in 1974.

9. Talstra I and II. Largely because of these two articles Schneider inserted some corrections and additions into the 5th edn of his grammar (1982).

10. Cf. Schneider §44.1.2; Talstra I, 169-70.

11. Schneider §44.1.2; 'zusammengesetzter Nominalsatz'; Talstra I, 169-70: 'complex nominal clause'.

12. Accepted in the 22nd-24th edition: cf. §§140f.

13. Gesenius-Kautzsch-Cowley §142a in respect of Gen. 3.13.

14. Meyer, III §92.4b.

15. W. Richter, *Grundlagen*, III, 10-11, note 22. See also other studies on syntax and grammar published in the series 'Arbeiten zu Text und Sprache im Alten Testament' (St. Ottilien: EOS Verlag) by Richter's own students. Now also W. Gross, *Die Pendenskonstruktion im biblischen Hebräisch*, St. Ottilien, 37-38, 190.

16. Note that אשר + QATAL, even though it has a finite verb form, is a nominal construction equivalent to article + participle. Actually, both occur in the protasis of the two-member syntactic construction. See the examples in §99.

17. J. Lyons, *Semantics*, Vol. 2, Cambridge, 1977, sections 11-12 can be consulted on this topic.

18. On this see H.J. Polotsky, 'Les transpositions du verbe en égyptien classique', *Israel Oriental Studies* 6 (1976) 1-50, especially §2.5, where the author compares Egyptian syntax with the syntax of other languages and also discusses the 'cleft sentence' in French ('c'est moi qui. . .').

19. On this topic see in particular Gross, *VTS* 32, 131-45. However, some of the points he defends will be modified in the following discussion.

20. Joüon §118c. The same opinion is held by Gesenius-Kautzsch §11a.

21. The problem is touched on by Gross, *VTS* 32, 132.

22. By this I mean the difficulty of defining the indivisible blocks of narrative in, for example, the Pentateuch-Joshua-Judges complex, in order to determine whether a beginning is relative or absolute.

23. Among the most recent solutions which can be consulted are B. Jongeling, 'Some Observations on the Beginning of Genesis I, 2', *Folia Orientalia* 21 (1980) 27-32: Gross, *VTS* 32, especially pp. 142-45; and now, by the same author, *Die Pendenskonstruktion*, 52-53. For discussions (both linguistic and theological) by mediaeval Jews consult S. Kamin, 'Rashbam's Conception of the Creation in the Light of the Intellectual Currents of His Time', in *Scripta Hierosolymitana* 31 (1986), 91-132 (especially pp. 122f.).

24. So already some mediaeval Hebrew scholars, including Rashi; cf. Gesenius-Kautzsch-Cowley §130d; Joüon §158d; E. König, *Syntax der hebräischen Sprache* (*Historisch-kritisches Lehrgebäude der hebräischen Sprache*, II.2) repr. Hildesheim-New York, 1972, §337 v-z, 421-23.

25. In syntactic structure, therefore, the first verses of Genesis are very like the opening sections of ancient near Eastern creation accounts (cf. Enuma elish, Egyptian texts and even elsewhere in the OT, for example Prov 8.24-26 'When there was not yet. . . then'). On this topic see E.A. Speiser, *Genesis*, Garden City, New York, 1964, 11-13; C. Westermann, *Genesis*, Neukirchen-Vluyn, 1974, 60-64.

26. In spite of the almost unanimous opinion of interpreters (cf. the discussion by B.S. Childs, *Introduction to the Old Testament as Scripture*, Philadelphia, 1979, 145-150) I maintain that 2.4 should not be split into two parts. Its construction is clearly chiastic and I do not think any subdivision is possible:

(a) אלה תולדות
(b) השמים
(c) והארץ
(d) בהבראם
(d) ביום עשות יהוה אלהים
(c) ארץ
(b) ושמים

'These were the origins of the sky and the land when they were created, on the day Yahweh made the land and the sky'. The central pair (d-d) reappears in almost identical form as part of another chiastic composition in 5.1-2:

(a) זה ספר תולדת אדם
(b) ביום ברא אלהים אדם
(c) בדמות אלהים עשה אתו
זכר ונקבה בראם
ויברך אתם

ויקרא את־שמם אדם
(b) ביום הבראם

'This is the book of the origins of man. On the day God created man, in God's image he made him, male and female he created them, he blessed them and called them man on the day they were created'. Since the pair occurs here as the outer frame of the chiastic pattern (b-b) it should mean that the '*tôledôt* formula' begins the section here whereas in 2.4 it is closural. Therefore, the account of creation extends from 1.1 to 2.4 and the so-called 'second account of creation' (in many ways an unfortunate expression!) does not begin in 2.4b but in 2.5. For various theories concerning the syntactic analysis of 2.4b-7 see now Gross, *Pendenskonstruktion*, 53-55.

27. Cf. the examples cited by Gross, *VTS* 32, 132, notes 5-6.

28. H.J. Polotsky, 'A Note on the Sequential Verb-Form in Ramesside Egyptian and in Biblical Hebrew', in S. Israelit-Groll, ed., *Pharaonic Egypt, the Bible and Christianity*, Jerusalem, 1985, 157-61.

29. Cf. Schneider, §48.3.

30. Termed 'Sprosserzählung' by Schneider, 200, 'embedded story' by Talstra I, 172, 173.

31. Cf. Schneider §54.2; Talstra I, 173. See also the study by E. König, 'Syntaktische Exkurse zum Alten Testament, 3', *ZAW* 19 (1899), 259ff.

32. This phrase should be connected with לא המיתו in spite of the Masoretic division.

33. The term 'Wiederaufnahme' or resumptive repetition, coined by H.W. Wiener, was used by C. Kuhl (*ZAW* 64 [1952] 1-11) as a principle of literary criticism to isolate the biblical sources. Recently his position has been corrected by S. Talmon, 'The Representation of Synchroneity and Simultaneity in Biblical Narrative', *Scripta Hierosolymitana* 27 (1978) 9-26 and by A. Berlin, *Poetics and the Interpretation of Biblical Narrative*, Sheffield, 1983, 126-28, who explain the 'Wiederaufnahme' as a literary device in biblical narrative. According to Talmon WAYYIQTOL and WAW-x-QATAL, the two verb forms which occur with the function of a 'reprise', are equivalent to each other. It is now possible, however, to separate their tense equivalents along the lines of the present investigation in the following way:

(1) In 1 Sam. 30.3 news of arrival, already given in v. 1, is resumed by a WAYYIQTOL after the interruption by vv. 1b-2. Note that the news is completed only in v. 3 and so the value of that WAYYIQTOL is not succession but conclusion (§38). Another example of the same kind is 1 Sam. 28.4 which reiterates 28.1.

(2) In other cases, though, the event narrated is self-contained as part of a later reference (with a WAYYIQTOL) so that the WAW-x-QATAL which recalls it to the reader (recovered information and antecedent) has the value of a pluperfect. See the two examples given in §16 and also 1 Sam. 19.18a (which reiterates v. 12b) and 2 Sam. 13.38 (which reiterates v. 34).

(3) Finally, in other cases this kind of antecedent construction, WAW-x-

QATAL, is not a pluperfect because it refers to the same event, first by a simple mention and then resumed in expanded form after an interruption. An example is 1 Sam. 5.1 where וּפְלִשְׁתִּים לָקְחוּ אֵת אֲרוֹן הָאֱלֹהִים 'And now the Philistines seized the ark of God' recalls the information given in 4.11 in order to continue the account concerning the fate of the ark after the interruption dealing with Eli's death and his daughter-in-law giving birth (4.12-22). Another example is 2 Sam. 5.18: וּפְלִשְׁתִּים בָּאוּ 'Now then the Philistines had come' which resumes the information given in v. 17a after the brief interruption by v. 17b (David's flight).

In conclusion, the information that WAYYIQTOL reiterates belongs to the main line of narrative (degree zero) whereas the resumption by a WAW-x-QATAL (with a tense equivalent of 2 or 3) provides this information as an antecedent to the episode which then follows (recovered information).

34. Cf. Beyer §1; Bartelmus, 211ff.

35. 75 per cent of the examples, according to the calculations of Beyer, 53; cf. Bartelmus, 211, 215, 216.

36. The QATAL occurs 60 times according to Beyer's calculations (p. 54). See also Bartelmus, 213 (for QATAL-x) and 214 (for x-QATAL). 1 Sam. 23.6 (with x-QATAL in the apodosis) is a problematic text in literary terms but syntactically it is perfectly correct Another example of the same type is 1 Kgs 21.1. For the WAW-x-QATAL construction in the apodosis see the list in Bartelmus, 211-12, 215. Note, also, 1 Sam. 30.1 where WAW-x-QATAL is an antecedent construction in the apodosis (§29).

37. Such cases are extremely rare in prose but that is no reason for considering them to be mistakes as Beyer does (p. 52, note 2; cf. p. 59: 'ganz unhebräisch'). On this see E. König, 'Syntaktische Exkurse', *ZAW* 19 (1899) 268-69 and Bartelmus, 214, note 20.

38. Weinrich, 11: 'Ein Text ist eine sinnvolle (d.h. kohärente und konsistente) Abfolge sprachlicher Zeichen zwischen zwei auffälligen Kommunikationsunterbrechungen'.

39. Cf. Joüon §118i and §§75, 140 below.

40. Joüon §118d.

41. Joüon, ibid., note 2.

42. Gesenius-Kautzsch-Cowley §72t.

43. Cf. BHS.

44. Cf. Beyer, 45-46.

45. Cf. Joüon §157d. Literally: 'they saw the face of Moses: that the skin of Moses' face was radiant'. For the construction cf. Joüon §157d.

46. I may be permitted a brief comment on the meaning of this passage. In general, scholars correct v. 21 following the ancient versions: 'And he reduced the people to slaves...' However, I think that would spoil the composition of this passage. Joseph summons the people to the cities because the grain was stored in them (41.48; cf. 41.35). In the cities he makes formal declaration that in Pharaoh's name he will buy the people themselves and

their lands and it is there that he distributes the seed and specifies how the harvest is to be distributed (47.23-26). It can be noted in passing that in v. 23 there is a special type of QATAL already noted in the classic grammars (e.g. Joüon §§112f.), which in modern terminology has been defined the 'performative', that is... 'hereby I buy you'. See, recently, P. Vernus, '"Ritual" *sḏm.n.f* and Some Values of the "Accompli" in the Bible and in the Koran', in Israelit-Groll, ed. *Pharaonic Egypt*, 307-316.

47. See, for example, Richter, *Grundlagen*, I, 99-101, for the distinction between long and short forms, and *Grundlagen*, II, 172, for the two negative constructions.

48. Schneider §51 and especially Talstra II, 30-31, both hint at the same meaning. Talstra defines clearly the first criterion set out above: 'If the verb (= YIQTOL) is in the first position, it will function as a jussive' (p. 31).

49. Talstra, II, 31, lists 'certain sequences of verbal forms' which should enable the jussive to be identified, but not all seem conclusive to me.

50. Cf. Beyer §4B2, pp. 238ff. ('Imperative + kai + Futurum').

51. The complements are expressed by the accusative: Gesenius-Kautzsch-Cowley, §117hh-ii.

52. See the glossary of technical terms in the appendix to M. Haran, *Temples and Temple Service in Ancient Israel*, Oxford, 1978, 349-365.

53. Note the division indicated by the *atnach* of the Massoretes, often ignored by translators!

54. Bendavid, II, 555ff.

55. Cf. Schneider §52.3-6; Talstra, I, 172.

56. Cf. Schneider §54; Talstra, I, 172-74.

57. The first is the inceptive form, the second the continuation form (for example, Gen. 37.9) with no obvious difference. The analysis by D. McCarthy, 'The Use of *wehinneh* in Biblical Hebrew', *Bib* 61 (1980) 330-42, concentrates on the form with WAW while S. Kogut, 'On the Meaning and Syntactical Status of *hinneh* in Biblical Hebrew', *Scripta Hierosolymitana* 31 (1986) 133-54 also examines the form without WAW. Kogut also discusses various opinions on the subject. As for the syntactic function of הנה, he does not seem to see any connection between the sentence introduced by this particle and what follows, at least not in the sense proposed by me. He is more interested in showing how הנה evolved through usage to absorb the verb ראה 'see!' with which it is often combined. Note that in my own discussion I will not consider cases where הנה is found in conjunction with a noun, pronoun or with elliptical sentences, on which see Kogut, *ibid.* 140-44.

58. Given by Bendavid, II, 529, 551.

59. Against *BHK* and *BHS*.

60. Note that הנה can also take the pronominal suffix, וְהִנּוֹ; see the examples in Bendavid, II, 553.

61. Bendavid, II, 555; cf. H.A. Brongers, 'Some Remarks on the Biblical Particle *hᵃlō*'', *OTS* 21 (1981) 180-85, where however this example is not cited.

62. A. Laurentin, '*We'attah—Kai nun*. Formule charactéristique des textes juridiques et liturgiques (à propos de Jean 17, 5)', *Bib* 45 (1964) 168-97; H.A. Brongers, 'Bemerkungen zum Gebrauch des adverbialen *we'attah* im Alten Testament', *VT* 15 (1965), 289-99.

63. Weinrich, 164.

64. Weinrich, Chapter 7.

65. Weinrich, Chapter 8.

66. Cf. Th. A. Busink, *Der Tempel von Jerusalem*, I, Leiden, 1970, 162ff.

67. See my review of B.O. Long, *I Kings*, Grand Rapids, 1984, in *LA* 34 (1984), 470-71.

68. Cf. Gross, *VTS* 32, 134.

69. Schneider, 199.

70. Cf. H. Haag, 'Der Aufstieg Josefs im Haus des Ägypters', in M. Görg, ed., *Fontes atque Pontes, Fs. Hellmut Brunner*, Wiesbaden, 1983, 205-14.

71. F.I. Andersen, *The Sentence in Biblical Hebrew*, The Hague–Paris–New York, 1974, has complained bitterly about this lack (pp. 17-18). Unfortunately, I was unable to follow his method or make use of his findings. Recently, E. Talstra, *II Kön. 3. Etüden zur Textgrammatik*, Amsterdam, 1983, has initiated a new approach by attempting to contrast Andersen's method with the method of W. Richter and his school (W. Gross and H. Schweizer).

72. Beyer §3.

73. See the list in Bartelmus, 216. Note that Gen. 24.15 (cited under 2b) is a complex nominal clause as טרם is preceded by the personal pronoun.

74. See the full discussion in §135 (Group II, nos. 11-13).

75. As well as in other texts cited by Joüon §176h, such as Lev. 22.30; 1 Kgs 8.64; Exod. 22.29.

76. Even without a preposition a noun denoting time can be used adverbially: cf. Gesenius–Kautzsch–Cowley §100c.

77. Beyer, 66.

78. For example, Meyer, III, 14; Schneider §44.4.4, 166; Talstra, I, 170. See also W. Gross, 'Zum Problem der Satzgrenzen im Hebräischen—Beobachtungen und Pendenzkonstruktionen', *BiblNot* 35 (1986), 50-72 as well as the monograph by the same author discussed in note 78.

79. As Joüon §156 suggests; recently also Muraoka, Chapter 6, confusing it with the complex nominal clause: cf. §§135-137, below. See also note 81.

80. On this topic cf. now Gross, *Pendenskonstruktion*, 64-77 who discusses the opinion of G. Vanoni (see note 83, below) and Bartelmus.

81. In the following discussion I have not been able to take into account Gross, *Pendenskonstruktion*, published only very recently. From a first

perusal it seems to me that alongside several similarities three main differences can be registered. (1) Gross speaks of '(a) construction with pendens' since he does not admit that a compound nominal clause (CNC) is involved and here I agree. I also agree that 'pendens' and accompanying sentence ('zugehöriger Satz') form a unit. But then the differences begin. For Gross it comprises a single clause; for me, two ('pendens' = protasis, connected clause = apodosis) which complement each other in the framework of a paragraph. That is why the WAW occasionally found in this construction is, for Gross, a marker ('Satzweiser') which only resembles the limit of a sentence ('Satzgrenze') but in actual fact has no such function. In my opinion, though, it is a WAW of apodosis, according to traditional terminology. (2) For Gross the associated sentence is syntactically complete when it contains a 'copy' of the 'pendens'. I agree, (even when the 'pendens' has no grammatical resumption) except that syntactically it is not independent because its component verb forms (or constructions) are non-initial (see text, below, under 2). (3) According to Gross the most important (even if not exclusive) stylistic function of the 'construction with pendens' is emphasis. In my opinion this never occurs. For emphasis, a category linked with the single sentence, Hebrew uses the CNC (see 3-4, below).

82. In Exod. 6.28 וירבר (29) ויהי ביום דבר יהוה אל־משה בארץ מצרים יהוה אל־משה לאמר, 'Now on the day on which Y. spoke to Moses in the land of Egypt, Y. spoke to Moses saying', the second member (main clause) is separated from the first (... ויהי) and is counted as a separate verse; also, the parasha begins in v. 29. This division is due, perhaps, to theological reasons (M. Greenberg, *Understanding Exodus*, New York, 1969, 137-38). But if v. 29 can stand alone, as grammatically it is a complete sentence, the same can be said of v. 28. In 2 Sam. 7.4, also, several manuscripts place a gap between the initial *wayehi*, which is a 'macrosyntactic sign' of narrative (§§28ff.) and the second, which is instead a 'strong' verb comprising the 'apodosis' (§30): cf. BHK and BHS. Different opinions regarding the nature of *wayehi* have been defended by G. Vanoni, 'Ist die Fügung *HYY* + Circumstanz der Zeit im Althebräisch ein Satz?', *BiblNot* 17 (1982), 73-86 and by J.P. Floss, 'Verbfunktionen der Basis *HYY*', *BiblNot* 30 (1985), 35-101.

83. I do not consider as completely proven Bartelmus' main thesis, namely that היה is always an 'empty' verb with no independent value, either lexically or semantically. See my comments in 'Esodo 3, 14a: "'Io sarò quello che ero" e un parallelo egiziano', *LA* 35 (1985), 7ff. especially p. 9 and note 11.

84. Cf. Meyer, III, 45: 'Hierbei handelt es sich wahrscheinlich um eine erstarrte Formel, die dazu dient, das Folgende als präterital auszuweisen'; Bartelmus, 114 (*Wayehi* is a 'Blosser Tempusmarker'). See Gross's discussion (cited in note 80).

85. Talstra I and II, passim.

86. This is similar to the view adopted by Bartelmus, 35-36.

87. At the theoretical level these assertions seem to be in agreement with

Bartelmus' position, 35-47. In his opinion the Hebrew verb system is based on categories of time ('Zeitlageverhältnis/Tempus') and from the way the action develops ('Ablaufsart', a term the author prefers to the more usual 'Aktionsart'). I maintain that Schneider is exaggerating when he denies the category 'Aktionsart' any validity (§48.7).

88. Weinrich, Chapter 3 (for the 'tenses') and Chapter 4 (for the 'mode' of action).

89. R.J. Williams, *Hebrew Syntax*, 2nd edn, Toronto–Buffalo–London, 1976, p. 3 and §§570ff.; Muraoka, Chapter 1.

90. Muraoka, 28, thinks differently as he does not accept the definitions of noun clause and verb clause given earlier, §6.

91. Cf. L. Köhler, 'Syntactica I', *VT* 2 (1952) 374-77: 'Syntactica III', *VT* 3 (1953), 188-89.

92. So also Muraoka, 31-34, though he proposes different solutions (see §138 below).

93. In this way, though, there is the risk of creating at one's desk forms and constructions which simply do not exist in the texts. To this category belong, for example, most of the 'exemples théoriques des formes verbales avec waw' provided by Joüon, 337.

94. Note that all the cases cited by Joüon §167a2 where YIQTOL or weYIQTOL of the protasis are in first position are poetic. In prose, though, the YIQTOL of the protasis is always in second position in normal cases where it is preceded by a conjunction (כִּי, אִם + YIQTOL) as well as in very rare cases where it occurs without a preposition (Num. 12.14; Judg. 13.12). It would seem, then, that in poetry the criterion of first position in the sentence, which is fundamental in prose, does not apply. This fact could provide an important key to understanding the verb system in poetry which still remains a mystery (§§171ff.).

95. Muraoka, 28ff. and Chapter 2.

96. Muraoka, 28-29.

97. Muraoka, 30. On the topic of spoken language J. Macdonald, 'Some Distinctive Characteristics of Israelite Spoken Hebrew', *BiOr* 32 (1975), 162-75, can be consulted especially pp. 163-66 on 'Inverted Word Order'. However, the author only makes comments of a general nature on the syntax of the verb and then mostly in connection with single sentences (cf. p. 174).

98. Unfortunately, Muraoka does not accept the distinction between verb clauses (V–S) and compound nominal clause (S–V) with the result that he has to resort to a series of special cases (pp. 34-36).

99. Cf. Joüon §18d.

100. Schneider, 189, note 9.

101. Gross, *VTS* 32, 133, note 7.

102. B. Johnson, *Hebräisches Perfekt und Imperfekt mit vorangehendem we*, Lund, 1979 has analysed the uses of weQATAL and weYIQTOL in

terms of the equivalent meanings and tenses in modern translations. It is a good collection of examples but compared with traditional grammars I do not think he has clarified the problem much.

103. Another difficult passage has been studied recently by R. Bartelmus, 'Ez. 37, 1-14, die Verbform *weqatal* und die Anfänge der Auferstehungshoffnung', *ZAW* 97 (1985) 366-89.

104. The use of the verb forms found to occur repeatedly in Joshua 15-19 (tribal borders) is quite normal. Each time the text begins with one or more WAYYIQTOL(s) notifying which territory has been allotted to the tribe in question. Then there is a pause in the narrative followed by a precise description of the borders in a series of weQATALs.

105. Accordingly, I do not think Gross is correct in maintaining that x-QATAL is a foreground construction in narrative (*VTS* 32, 138).

106. Watson, *Classical Hebrew Poetry*; see my review in *LA* 35 (1985) 471-73.

107. M. Dahood, 'Ugaritic-Hebrew Parallel Pairs', in L.R. Fisher, ed., *Ras Shamra Parallels*, I, Rome 1972, 71-382: II, 1975, 1-39; III, 1981, 1-206.

108. Y. Avishur, *Stylistic Studies of Word-Pairs in Biblical and Ancient Semitic Literatures*, Neukirchen-Vluyn, 1984.

109. His principle of emending the text, including the consonants, on the basis of attested word-pairs (cf. part III) should be viewed with caution.

110. W.R. Watters, *Formula Criticism and the Poetry of the Old Testament*, Berlin/New York, 1976.

111. For example, as applied to the book of Job (pp. 130-32).

112. In the 'Anchor Bible' series: Psalms I-III.

113. See the discussion by Dahood himself, *Psalms*, II, pp. XVII-XIX; III, p. XXVIII; also Watson, *Classical Hebrew Poetry*, 58.

114. Bibliography in Watson, *Classical Hebrew Poetry*, 58.

115. Regrettably, Watson, *Classical Hebrew Poetry*, 279-80, devotes only a few lines to the YIQTOL/QATAL and QATAL/YIQTOL variations in tense.

116. T. Fenton, 'The Hebrew Tenses in the Light of Ugaritic', *Proceedings of the Fifth World Congress of Jewish Studies*, IV, Jerusalem, 1973, 31-39.

117. U. Cassuto, *The Goddess Anath*, Jerusalem, 1971, 46-47 (the date of the original Hebrew is 1951).

118. M. Held, 'The *yqtl-qtl* (*qtl-yqtl*) Sequence of Identical Verbs in Biblical Hebrew and Ugaritic', in *Studies in Honor of Abraham A. Neuman*, Leiden, 1962, 190-281.

119. אונים abstract for concrete; Watson, *Classical Hebrew Poetry*, 314-16.

120. S. Gevirtz, 'Evidence of Conjugational Variation in the Parallellization of Selfsame Verbs in the Amarna Letters', *JNES* 32 (1973), 99-104.

121. For example, see the full list from the Psalter in Dahood, *Psalms*, III, 420-23.

122. W. Gross, *Verbform und Funktion*, wayyiqtol *für die Gegenwart?*, St. Ottilien, 1976.

123. Pp. 93-99 and 165 respectively.

ADDITIONAL BIBLIOGRAPHY

Andersen, F.I., *The Sentence in Biblical Hebrew*, The Hague–Paris–New York, 1974.

Avishur, Y., *Stylistic Studies of Word-Pairs in Biblical and Ancient Semitic Literatures*, Neukirchen-Vluyn, 1984.

Bartelmus, R., 'Ez 37,1-14, die Verbform $w^e qatal$ und die Anfänge der Auferstehungshoffnung', *ZAW* 97 (1985), 366-89.

Bendavid, A., *Parallels in the Bible*, Jerusalem, 1972.

Berlin, A., *Poetics and Interpretation of Biblical Narrative*, Sheffield, 1983.

Brongers, H.A., 'Bemerkungen zum Gebrauch des adverbialen $w\check{e}{}^{c}att\hat{a}h$ im Alten Testament', *VT* 15 (1965), 289-99.

—'Some Remarks on the Biblical Particle $h^a l\bar{o}$', *OTS* 21 (1981), 180-85.

Busink, Th. A., *Der Tempel von Jerusalem*, I, Leiden, 1970.

Cassuto, U., *The Goddess Anath*, Jerusalem, 1971.

Childs, B.S., *Introduction to the Old Testament as Scripture*, Philadelphia, 1979.

Dahood, M., *Psalms*, I-III, Garden City, New York, 1966-1970.

—'Ugaritic-Hebrew Parallel Pairs', in L.R. Fisher, ed., *Ras Shamra Parallels*, I, Roma, 1972, 71-382; II, 1975, 1-39.

Fenton, T., 'The Hebrew Tenses in the Light of Ugaritic', in *Proceedings of the Fifth World Congress of Jewish Studies*, IV, Jerusalem, 1973, 31-39.

Floss, J.P., 'Verbfunktionen der Basis *HYY*', *BiblNot* 30 (1985), 35-101.

Gevirtz, S., 'Evidence of Conjugational Variation in the Parallelization of Selfsame Verbs in the Amarna Letters', *JNES* 32 (1973), 99-104.

Greenberg, M., *Understanding Exodus*, New York, 1969.

Gross, W., *Die Pendenskonstruktion im Biblischen Hebräisch*, St. Ottilien, 1987.

Gross, W., 'Zum Problem der Satzgrenzen im Hebräischen—Beobachtungen an Pendenskonstruktionen', *BiblNot* 35 (1986), 50-72.

—*Verbform und Funktion. wayyiqtol für die Gegenwart?*, St Ottilien, 1976.

Haag, H., 'Der Aufstieg Josefs im Haus des Ägypters', in M. Görg, ed., *Fontes atque Pontes, Fs. Hellmut Brunner*, Wiesbaden, 1983, 205-14.

Haran, M., *Temples and Temple Service in Ancient Israel*, Oxford, 1978.

Held, M., 'The *yqtl-qtl* (*qtl-yqtl*) Sequence of Identical Verbs in Biblical Hebrew and Ugaritic', in *Studies in Honor of Abraham A. Neuman*, Leiden, 1962, 281-90.

Israelit-Groll, S., ed., *Pharaonic Egypt, the Bible and Christianity*, Jerusalem, 1985.

Johnson, B., *Hebräisches Perfekt und Imperfekt mit vorangehendem* w^e, Lund, 1979.

Jongeling, B., 'Some Observations on the Beginning of Genesis I, 2', *Folia Orientalia* 21 (1980), 27-32.

Kamin, S., 'Rashbam's Conception of the Creation in the Light of the Intellectual Currents of His Time', *Scripta Hierosolymitana* 31 (1986), 91-132.

Kogut, S., 'On the Meaning and Syntactical Status of *hinnēh* in Biblical Hebrew', *Scripta Hierosolymitana* 31 (1986), 133-54.

Köhler, L., 'Syntactica I', *VT* 2 (1952), 374-77.

—'Syntactica III', *VT* 3 (1953), 188-89.

König E., 'Syntactische Excurse zum Alten Testament, 3', *ZAW* 19 (1899), 259-87.
—*Syntax der hebräischen Sprache* (Historisch-kritisches Lehrgebäude der hebräischen Sprache, II.2), repr. Hildesheim–New York, 1979.
Laurentin, A., '*We'attâh - Kai nun*. Formule caractéristique des textes juridiques et liturgiques (à propos de Jean 17,5)', *Bib* 45 (1964), 168-97.
Long, B.O., *1 Kings*, Grand Rapids, 1984.
Lyons, J., *Semantics*, Volume 2, Cambridge 1977.
Macdonald, J., 'Some Distinctive Characteristics of Israelite Spoken Hebrew', *BiOr* 32 (1975), 162-75.
McCarthy, D., 'The Use of *wᵉhinnēh* in Biblical Hebrew', *Bib* 61 (1980), 330-42.
McFall, L., *The Enigma of the Hebrew Verbal System*, Sheffield, 1982.
Müller, H.-P., 'Ebla und das althebräische Verbalsystem', *Bib* 65 (1984), 145-67.
—'Zur Geschichte des hebräischen Verbs—Diachronie der Konjugationsthemen', *BZ* 27 (1983), 34-57.
Niccacci, A., 'Esodo 3,14a: 'Io sarò quello che ero' e un parallelo egiziano', *LA* 35 (1985), 7-26.
Polotsky, H.J., 'A Note on the Sequential Verb-Form in Ramesside Egyptian and in Biblical Hebrew', in Israelit-Groll, ed., *Pharaonic Egypt*, 157-61.
—'Les transpositions du verbe en égyptien classique', *Israel Oriental Studies* 6 (1976), 1-50.
Speiser, E.A., *Genesis*, Garden City, New York, 1964.
Talmon, S., 'The Representation of Synchroneity and Simultaneity in Biblical Narrative', *Scripta Hierosolymitana* 27 (1978), 9-26.
Talstra, E., *II Kön 3. Etüden zur Textgrammatik*, Amsterdam, 1983.
Thacker, T.W., *The Relationship of the Semitic and Egyptian Verbal Systems*, Oxford, 1954.
Vanoni, G., 'Ist die Fügung *HYY* + Circumstanz der Zeit im Althebräisch ein Satz?', *BiblNot* 17 (1982), 73-86.
Vernus, P., 'Ritual' *sdm.n.f* and Some Values of the 'Accompli' in the Bible and in the Koran', in Israelit-Groll, ed., *Pharaonic Egypt*, 307-16.
Watters, W.R., *Formula Criticism and the Poetry of the Old Testament*, Berlin–New York, 1976.
Westermann, C., *Genesis*, Neukirchen-Vluyn, 1974.
Williams, R.J., *Hebrew Syntax*, Toronto–Buffalo–London, 1976.
Züber, B., *Das Tempussystem des biblischen Hebräisch*, Berlin–New York, 1986.

INDEXES

INDEX OF BIBLICAL REFERENCES

INDEX OF AUTHORS

JOURNAL FOR THE STUDY OF THE OLD TESTAMENT

Supplement Series

* (Out of Print)